The INNOVATIVE ART WORKS of
Sarah Bryant

The INNOVATIVE ART WORKS of
Sarah Bryant

A Collection of Unique Hand Drawn Designs

Rev. date: 08/04/2015

To order additional copies of this book, contact:
Xlibris
1-800-455-039
www.Xlibris.com.au
Orders@Xlibris.com.au
721220

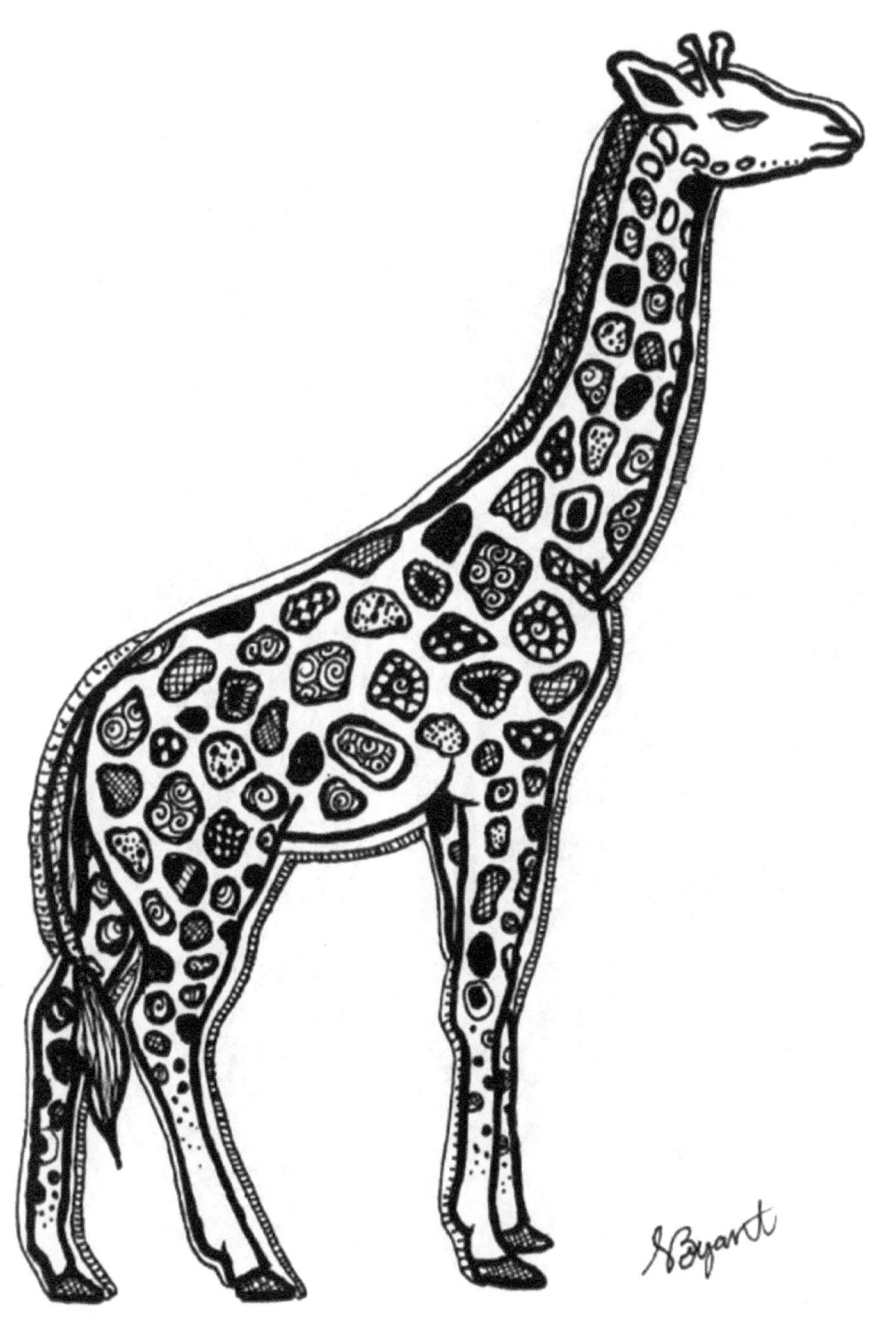

A Collection of Spots

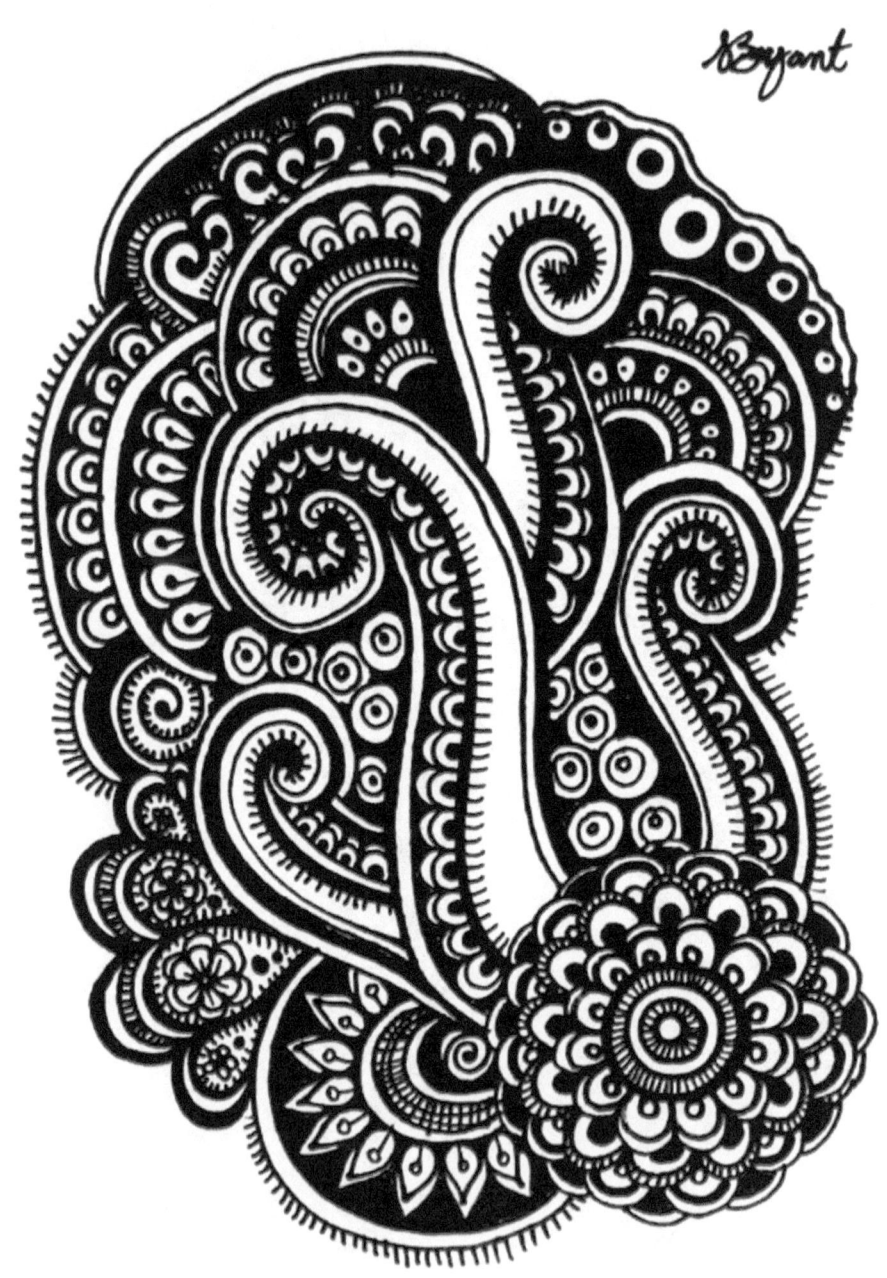

A Lyre's Tail

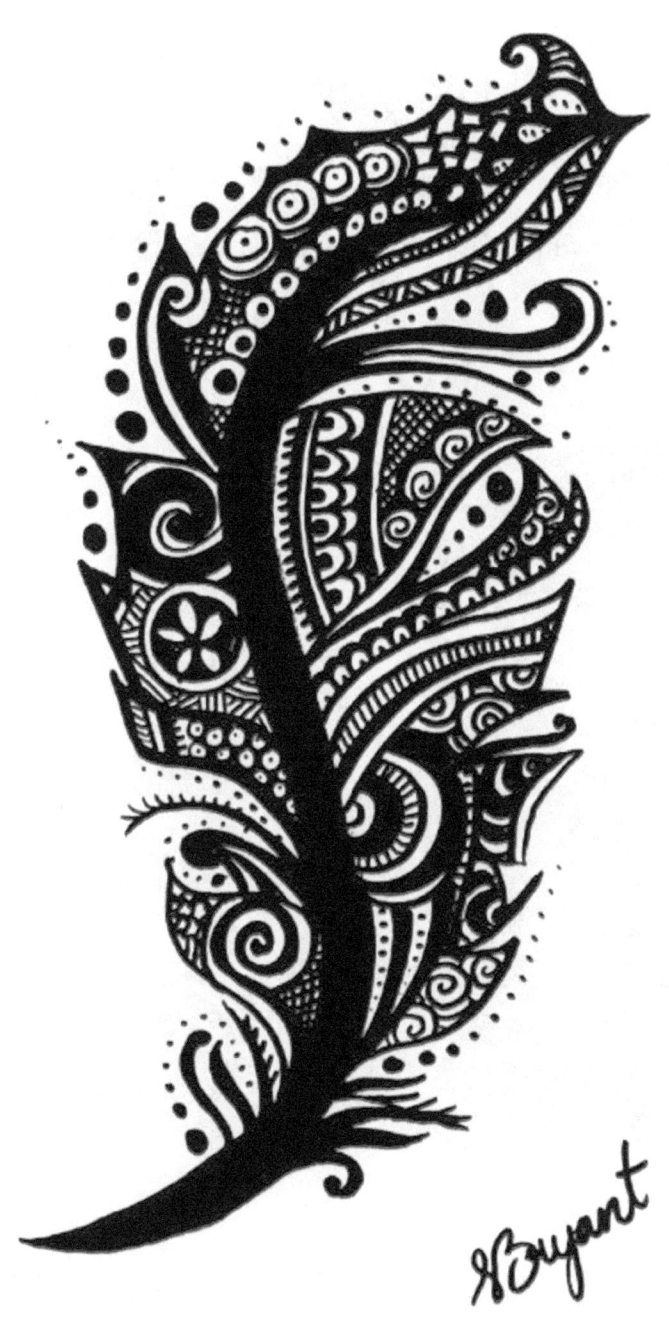

As Light as a Feather

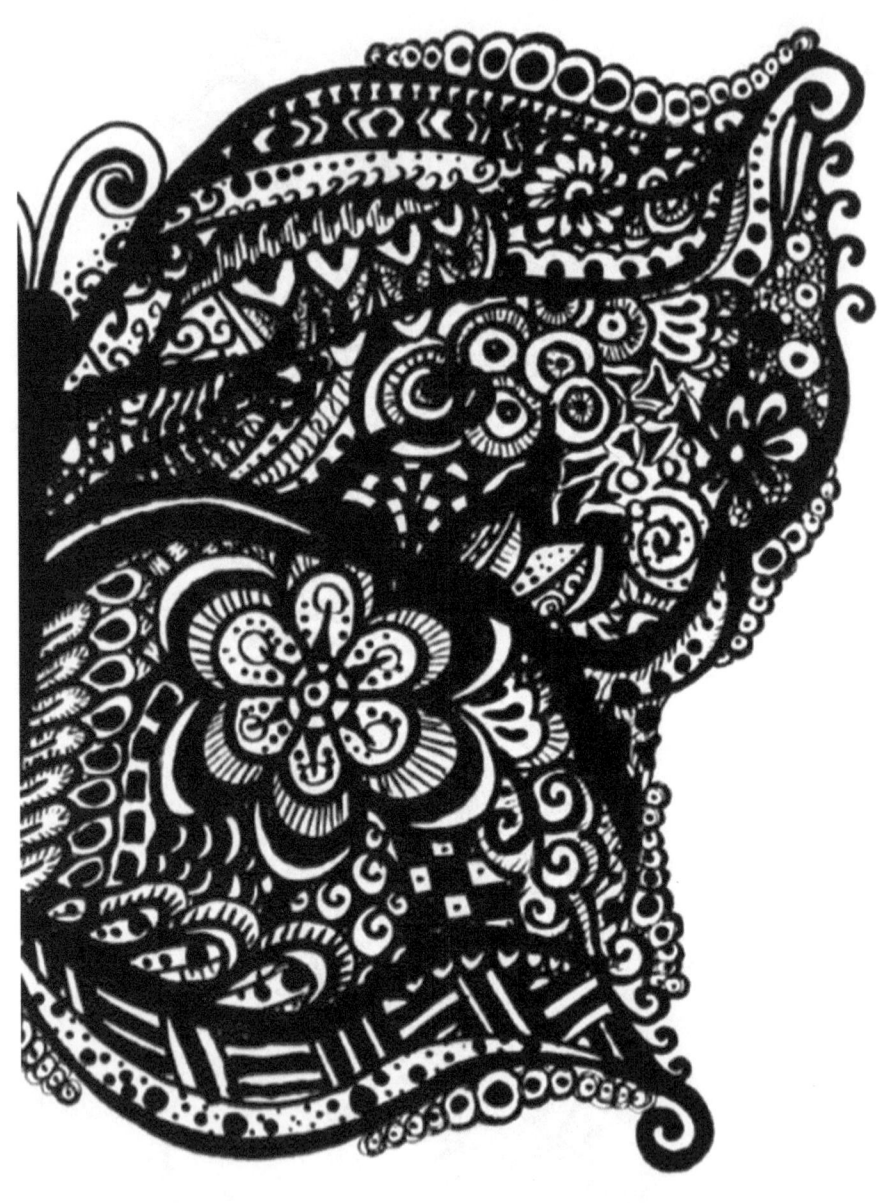

Beauties of a Butterfly's Wing

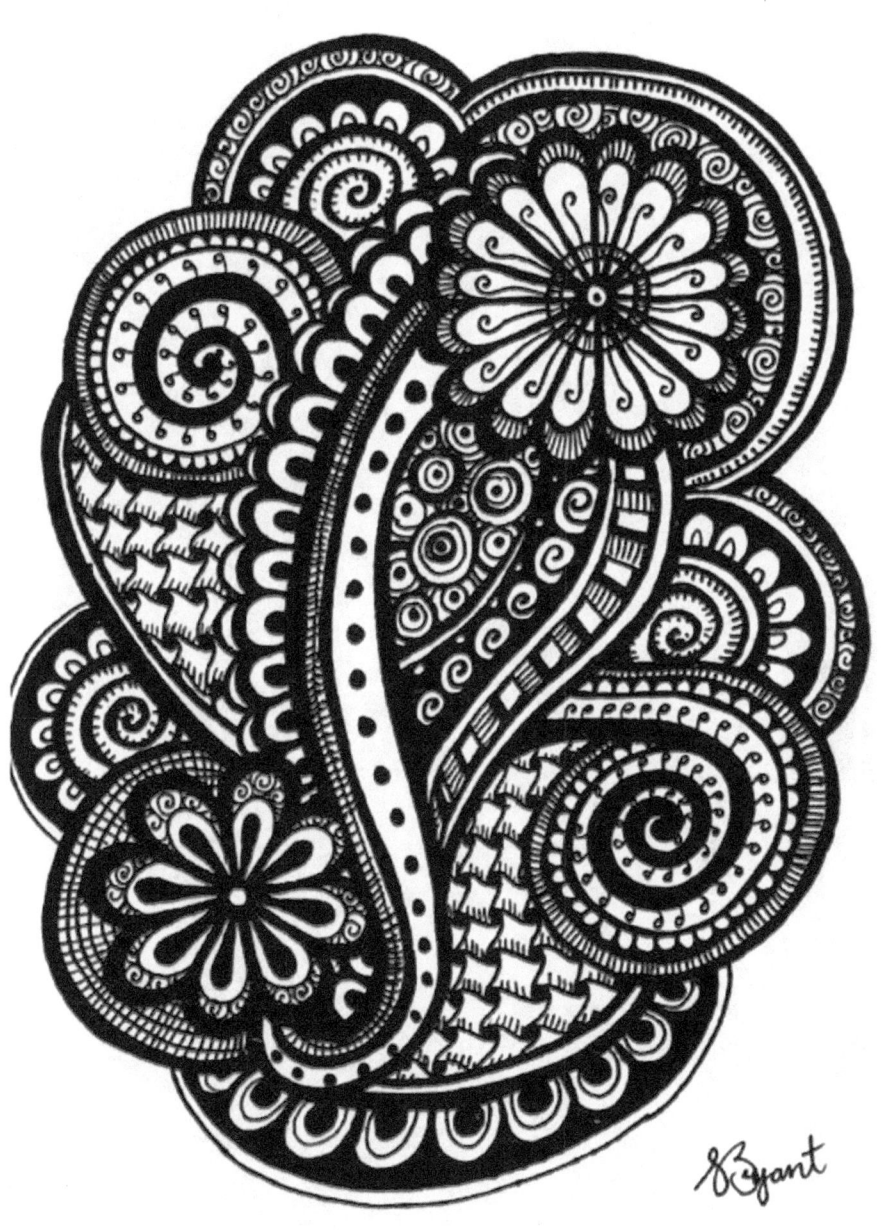

Beautiful and Bold

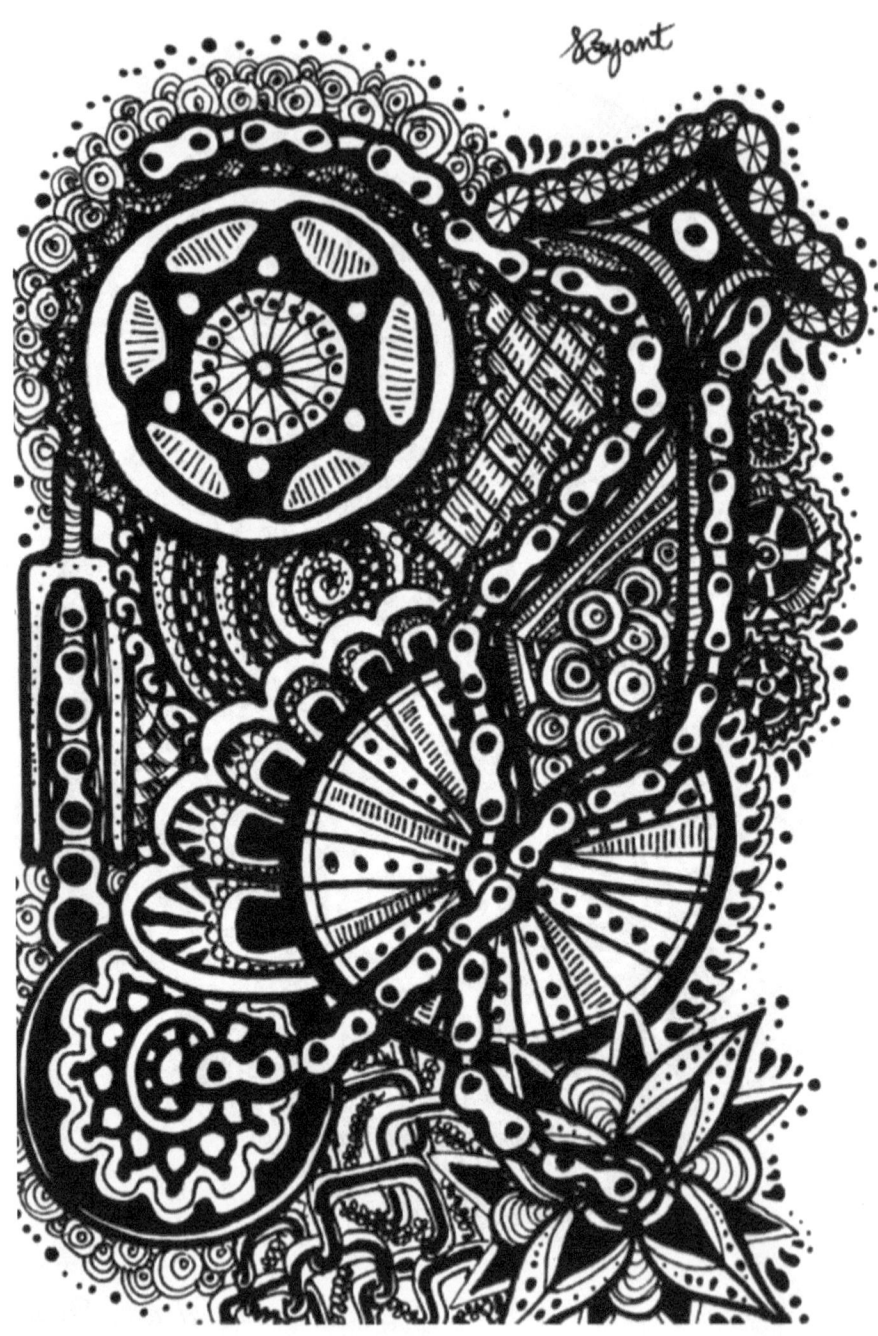

Bike Mechanics

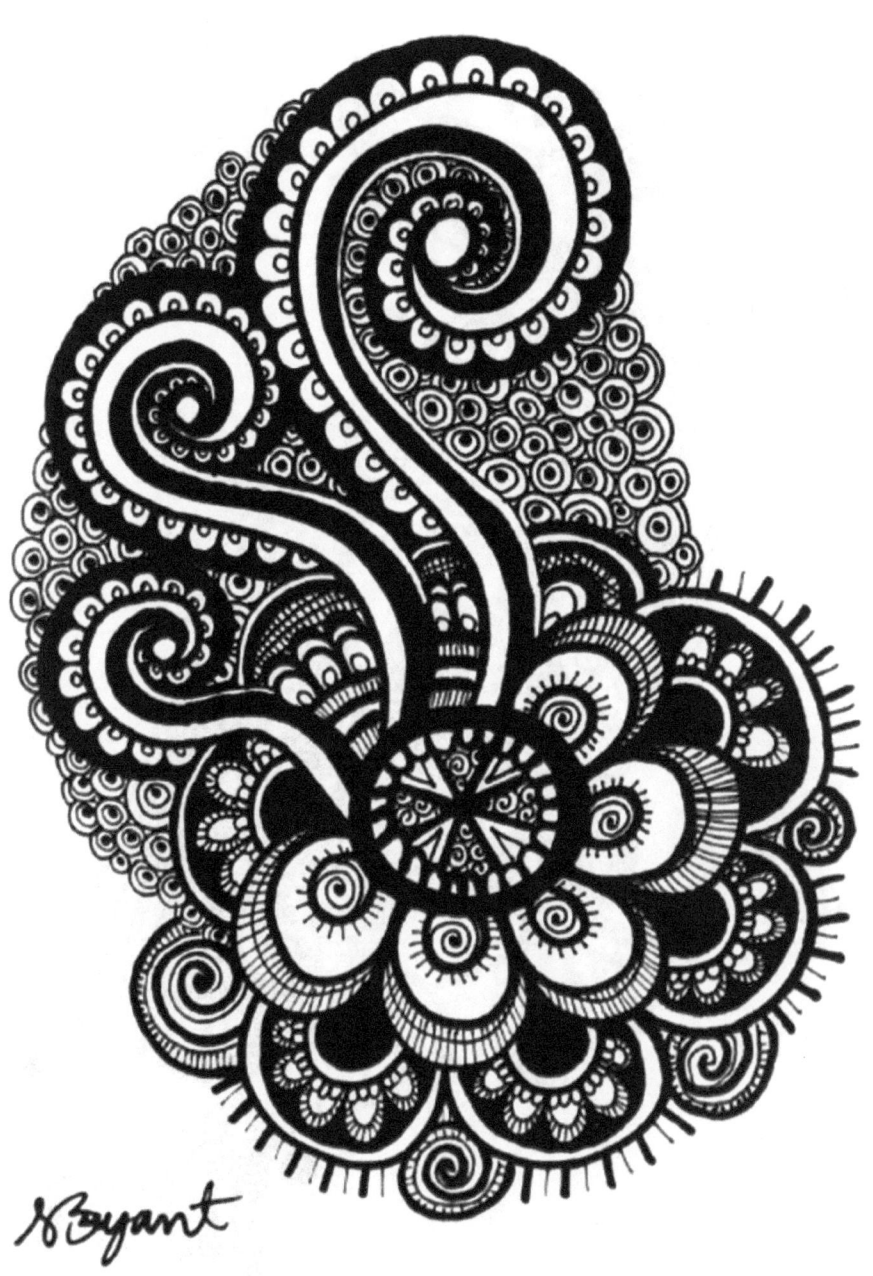

Bubbles

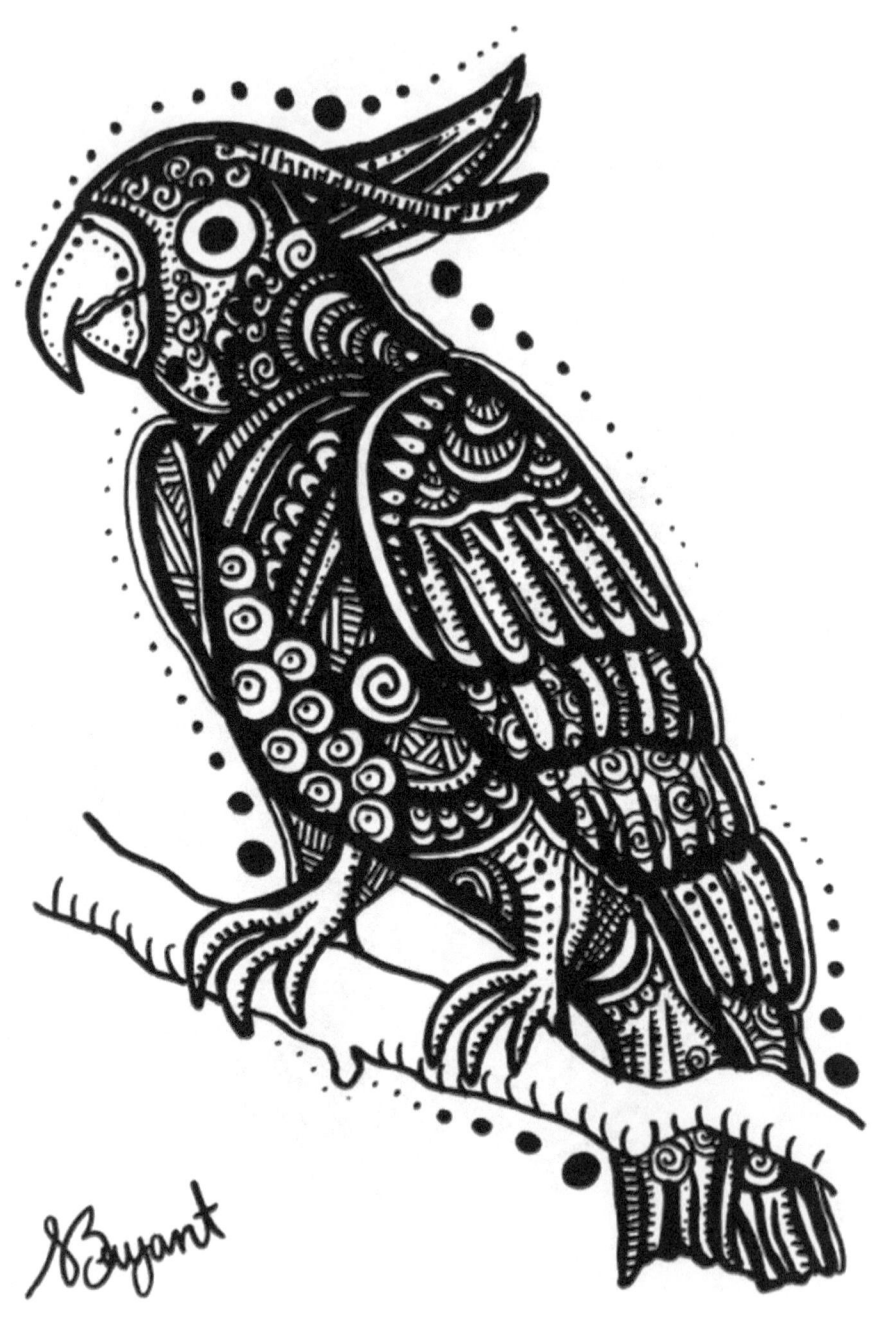

Cacatuidae Cockatoo

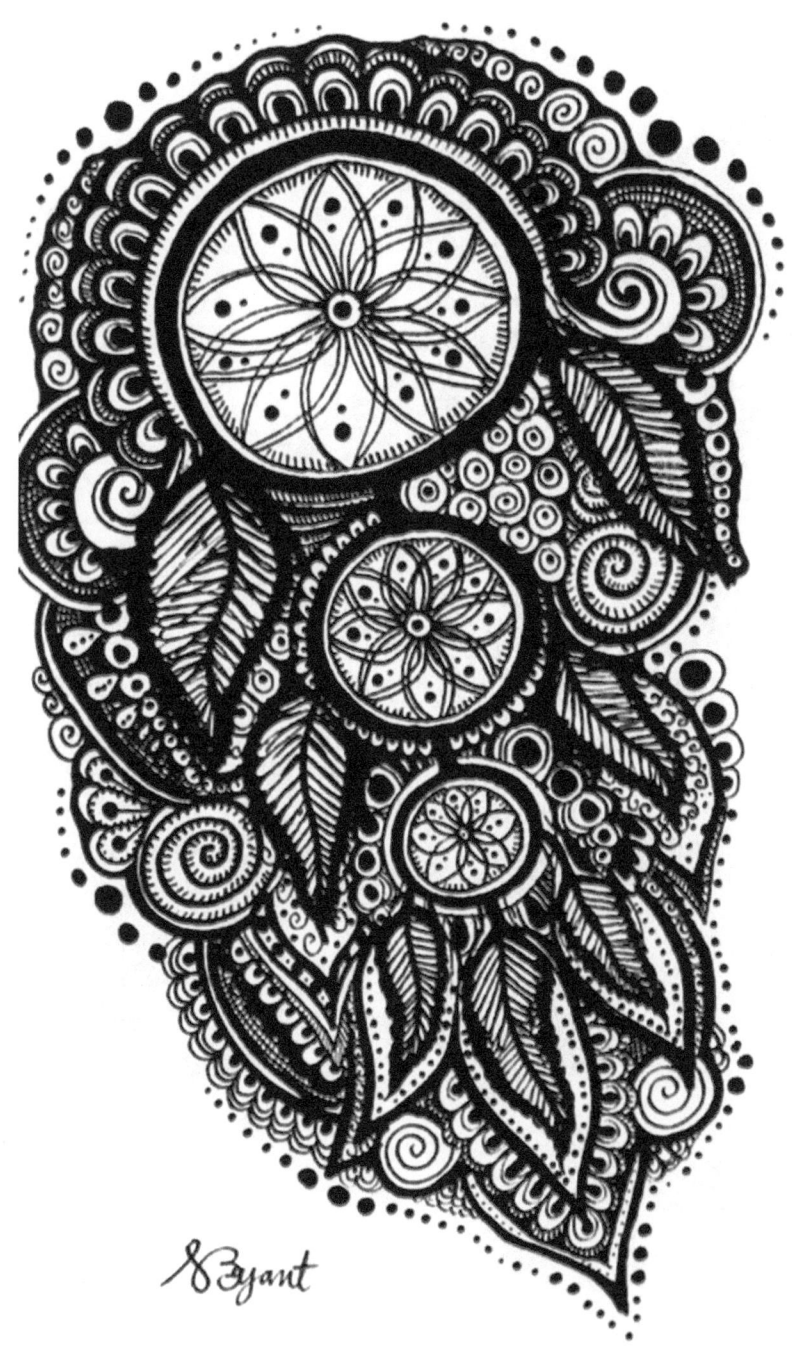

S Bryant

Catcher of Dreams

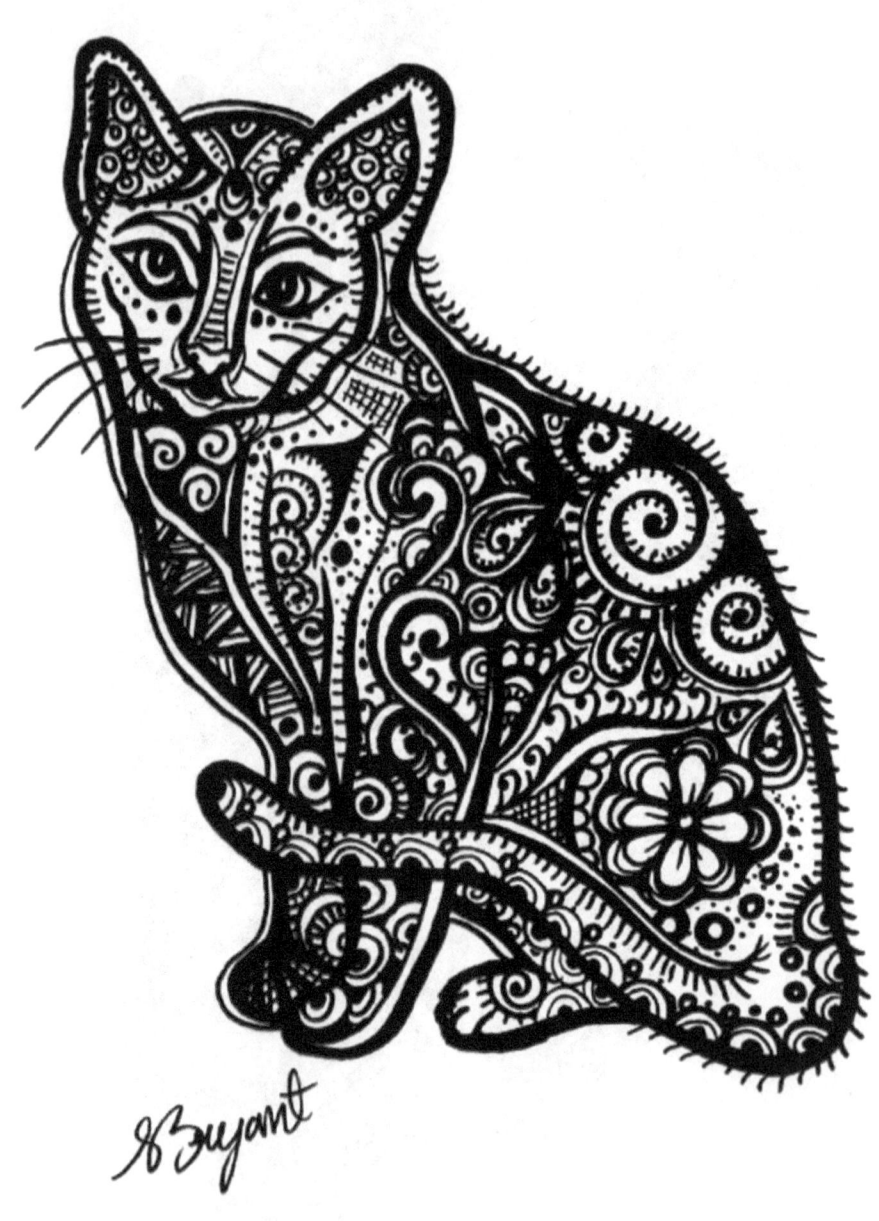

Catlike

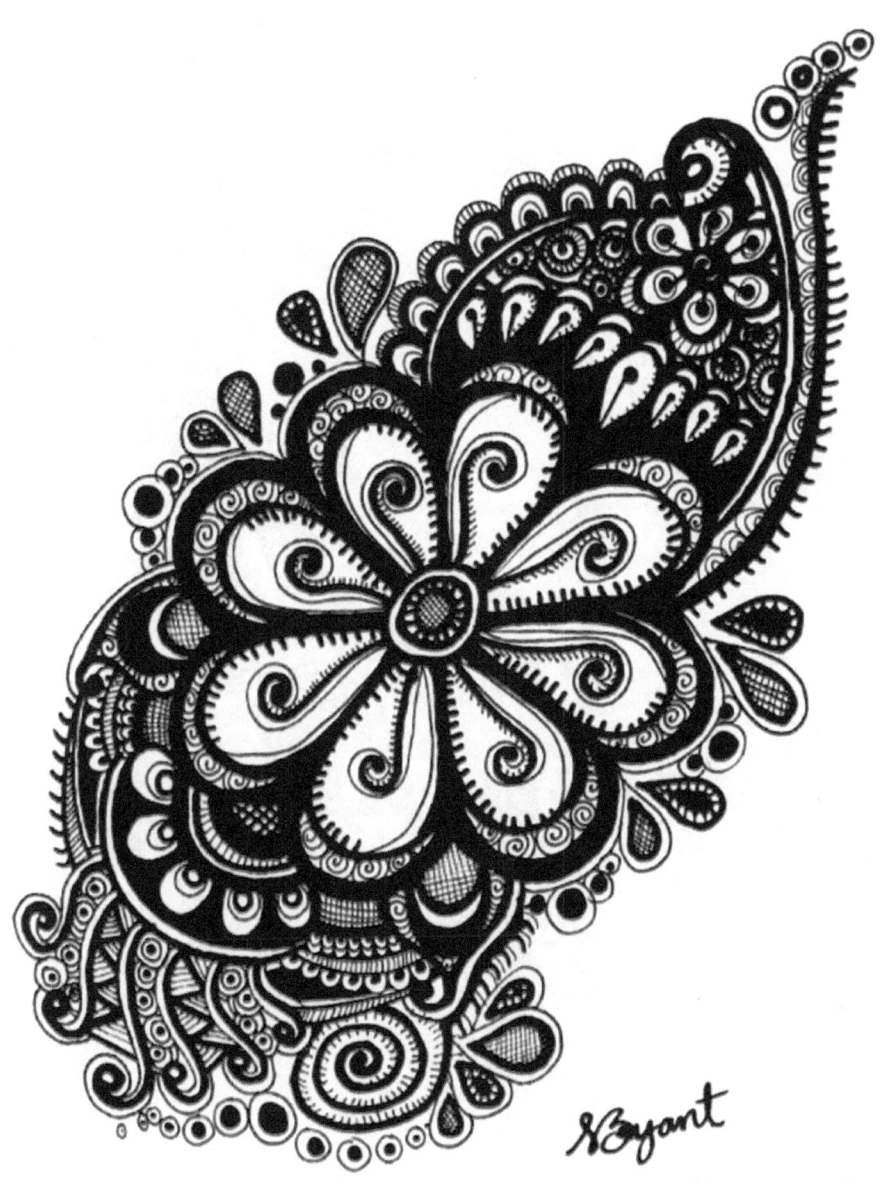

Crescita Fiore (Flower Growth)

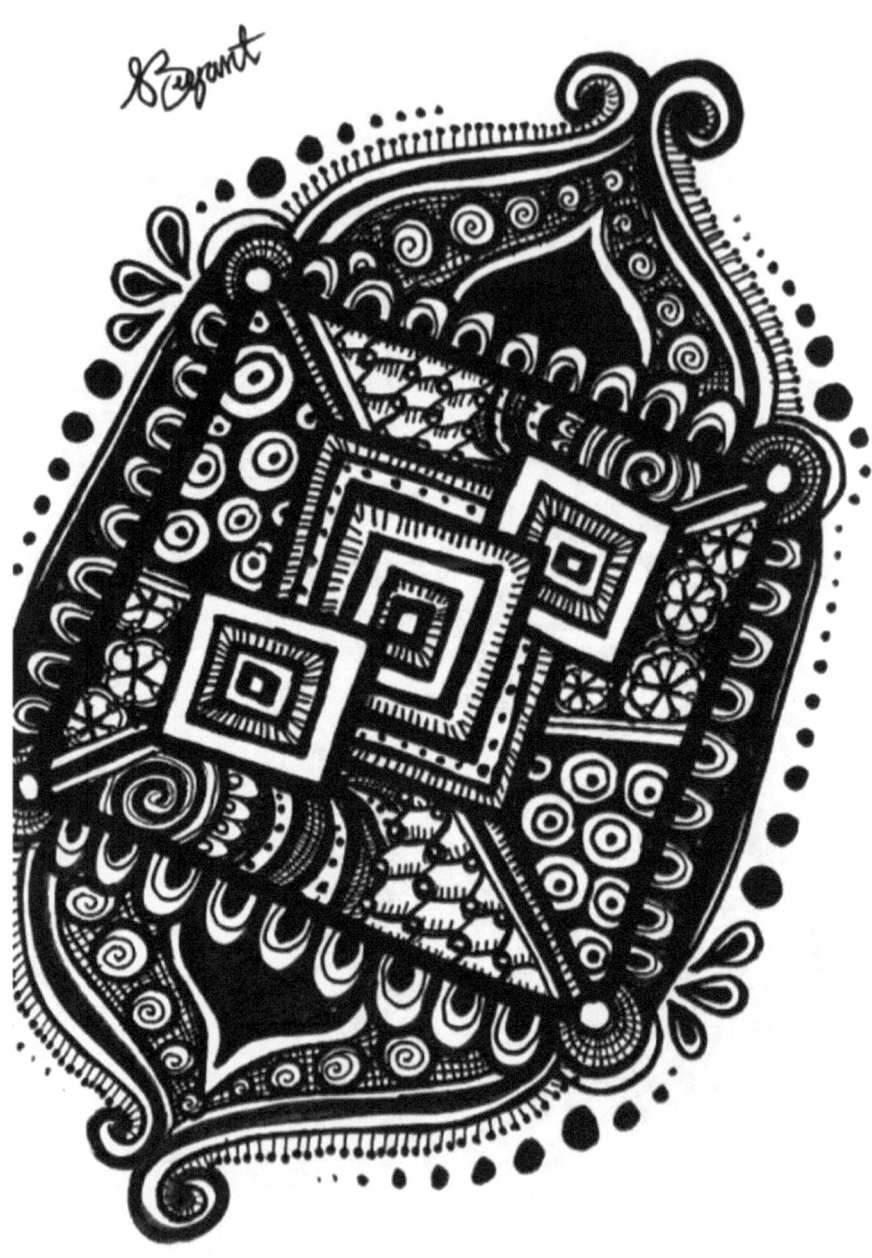

Cubed

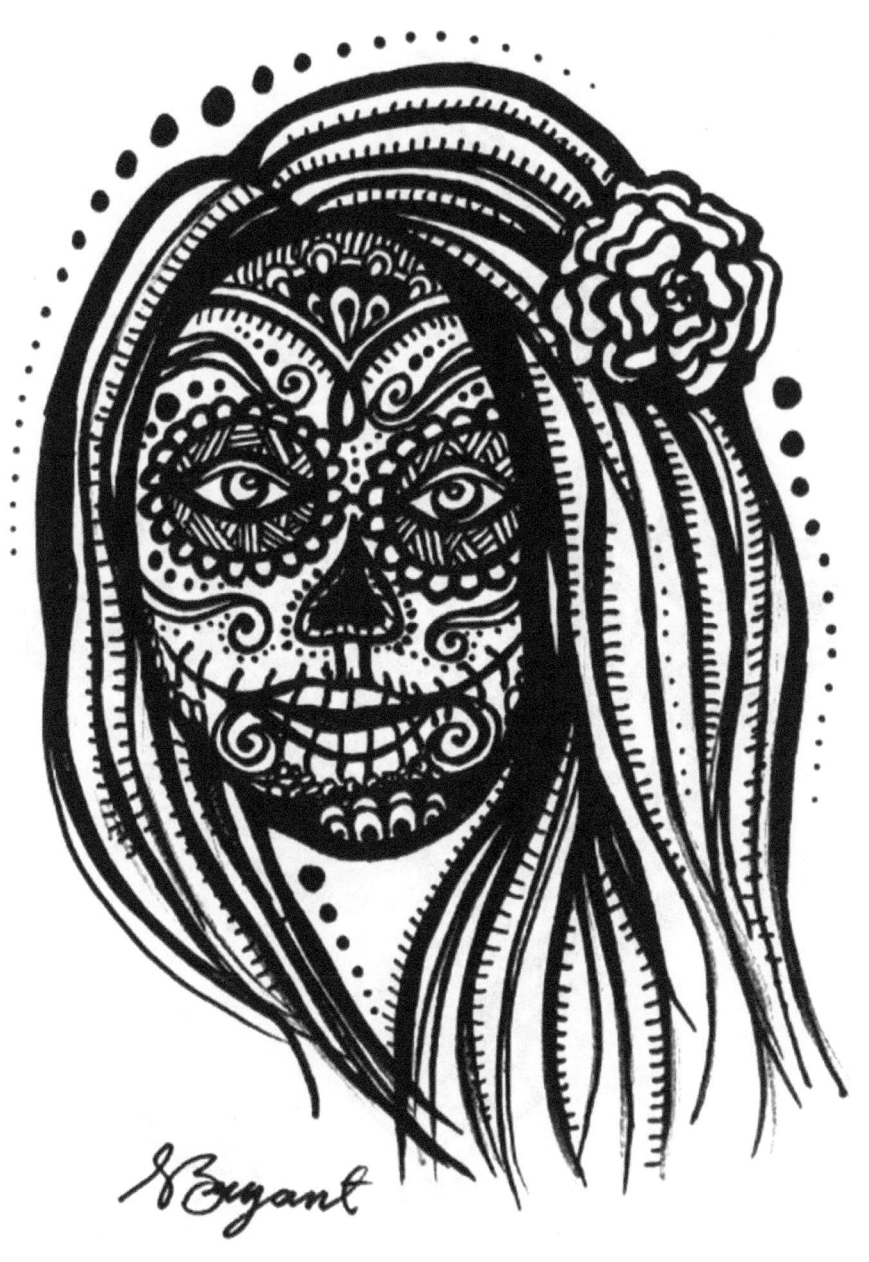

Day of the Dead Girl

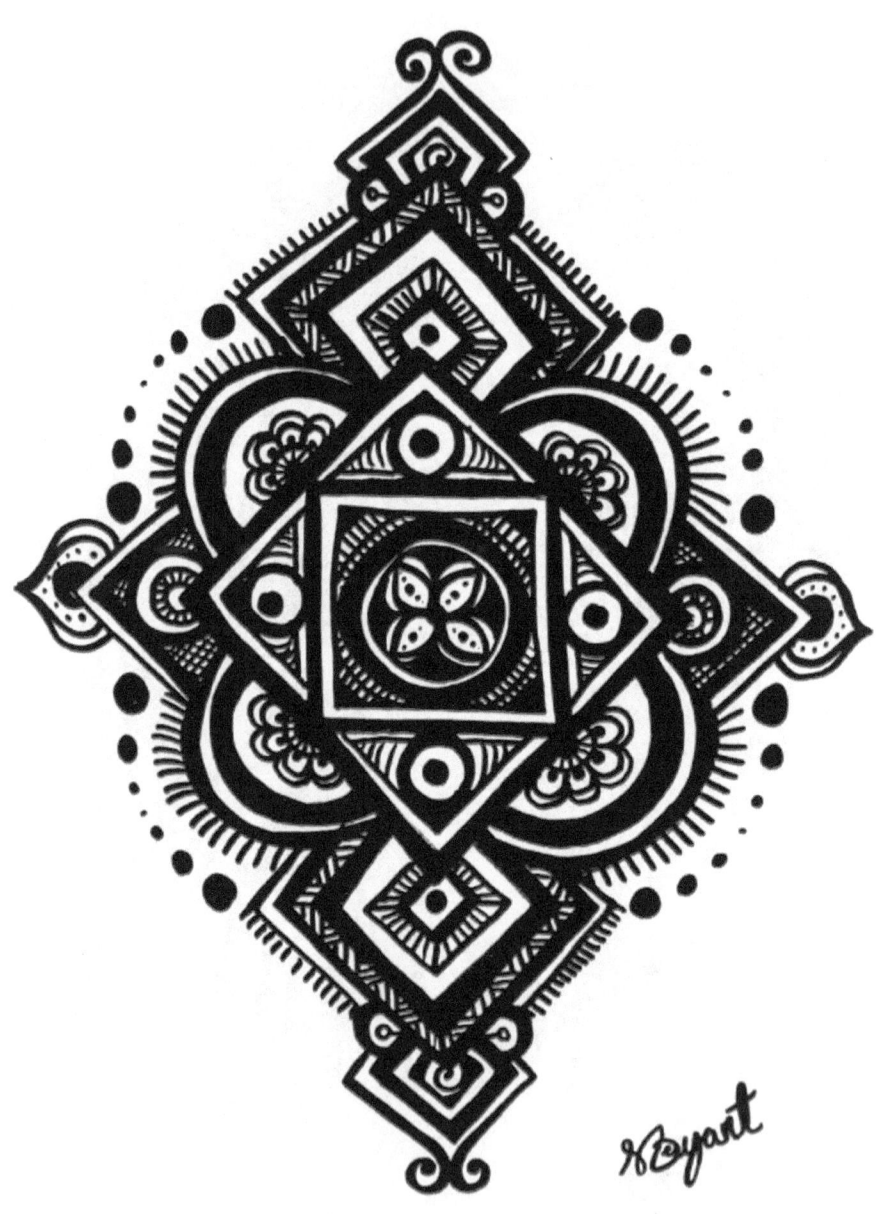

Delicate Diamonds

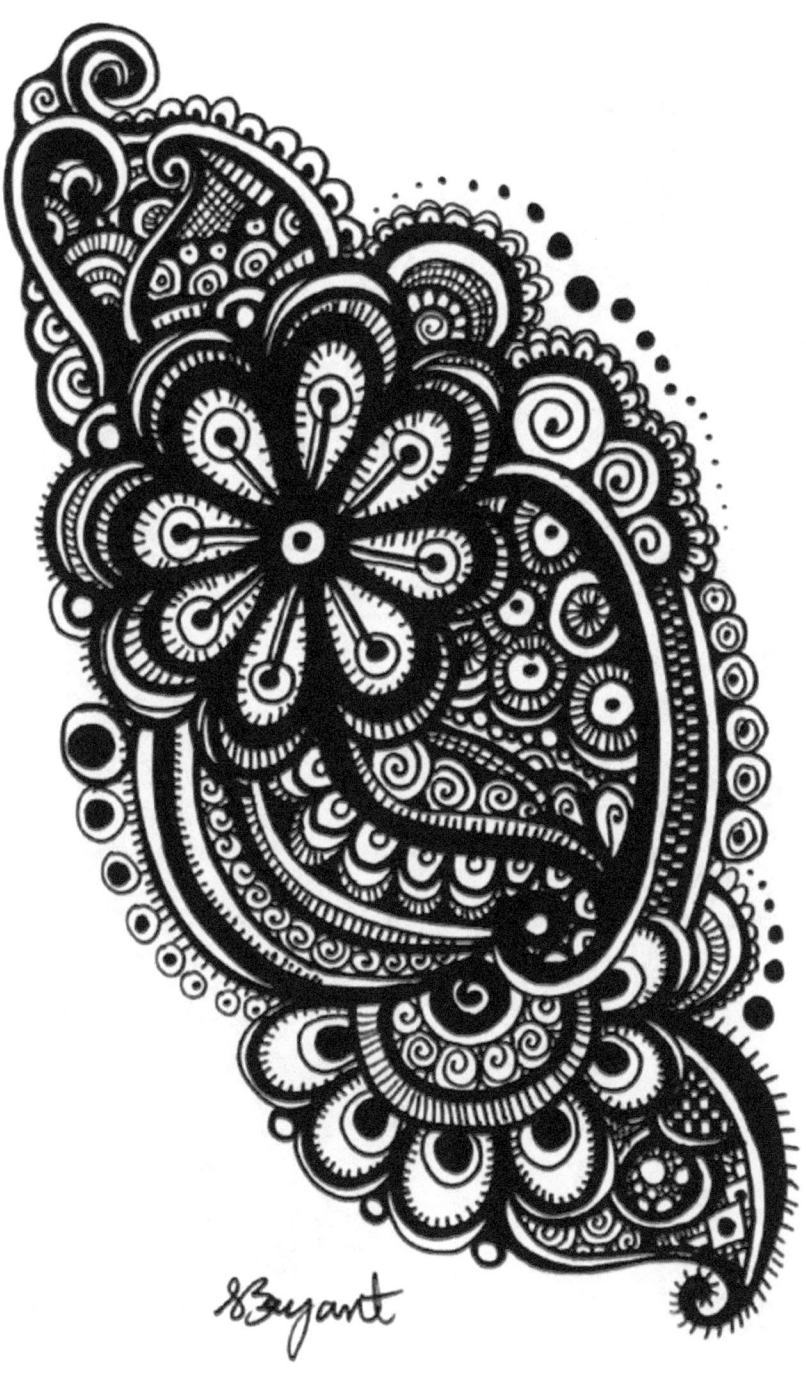

Bryant

Drops

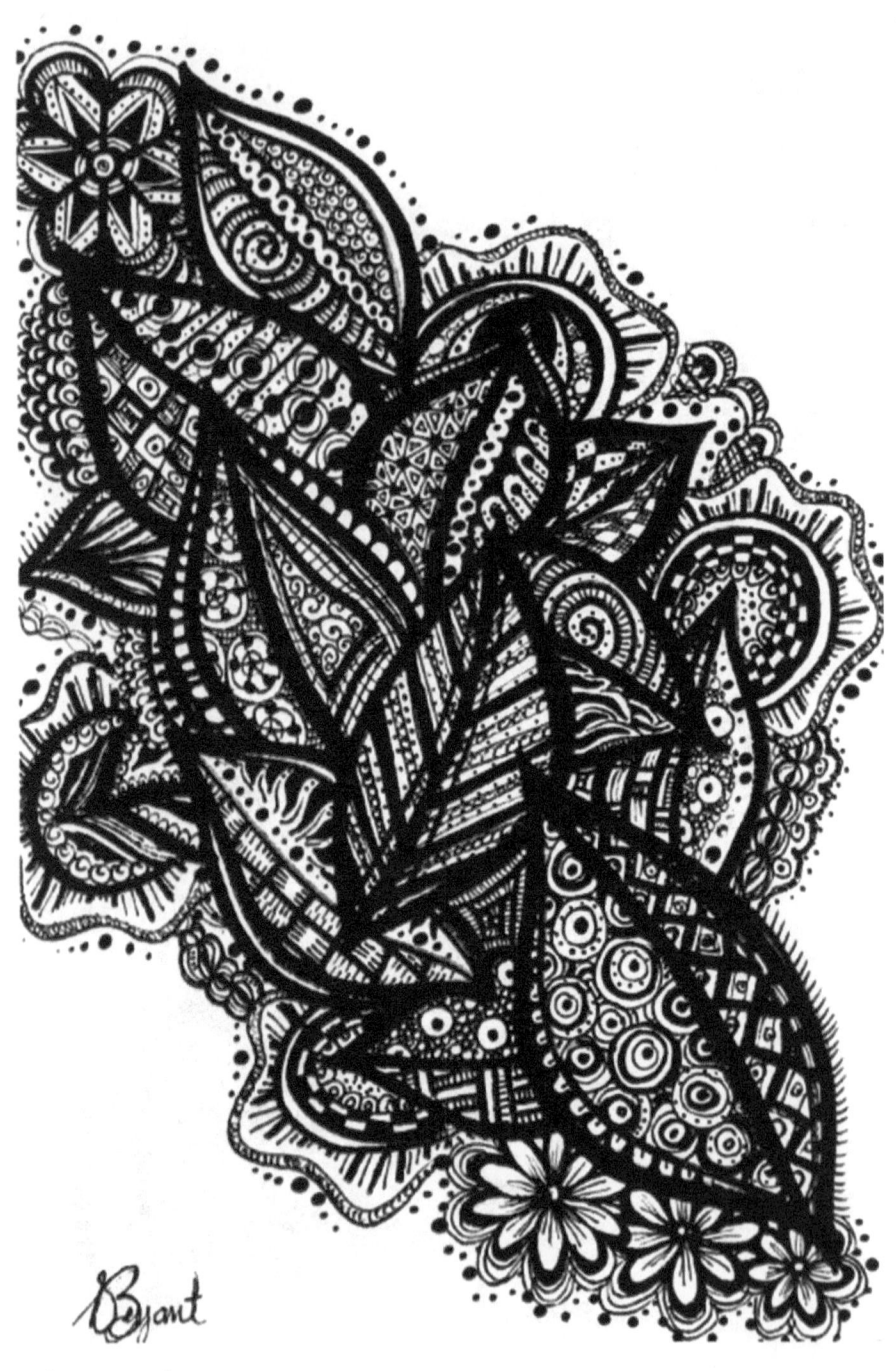

Bryant

Falling Leaves

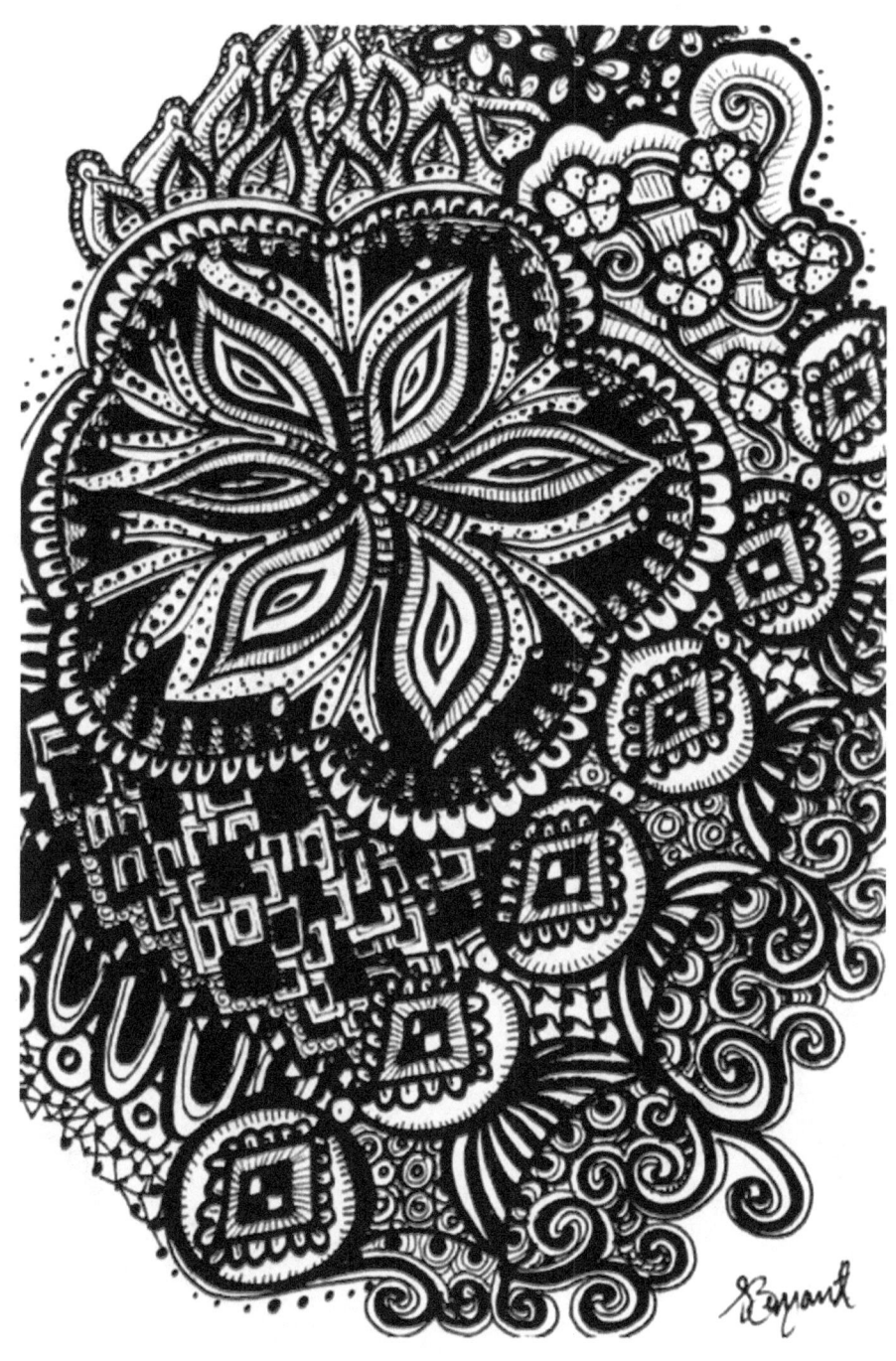

Flame

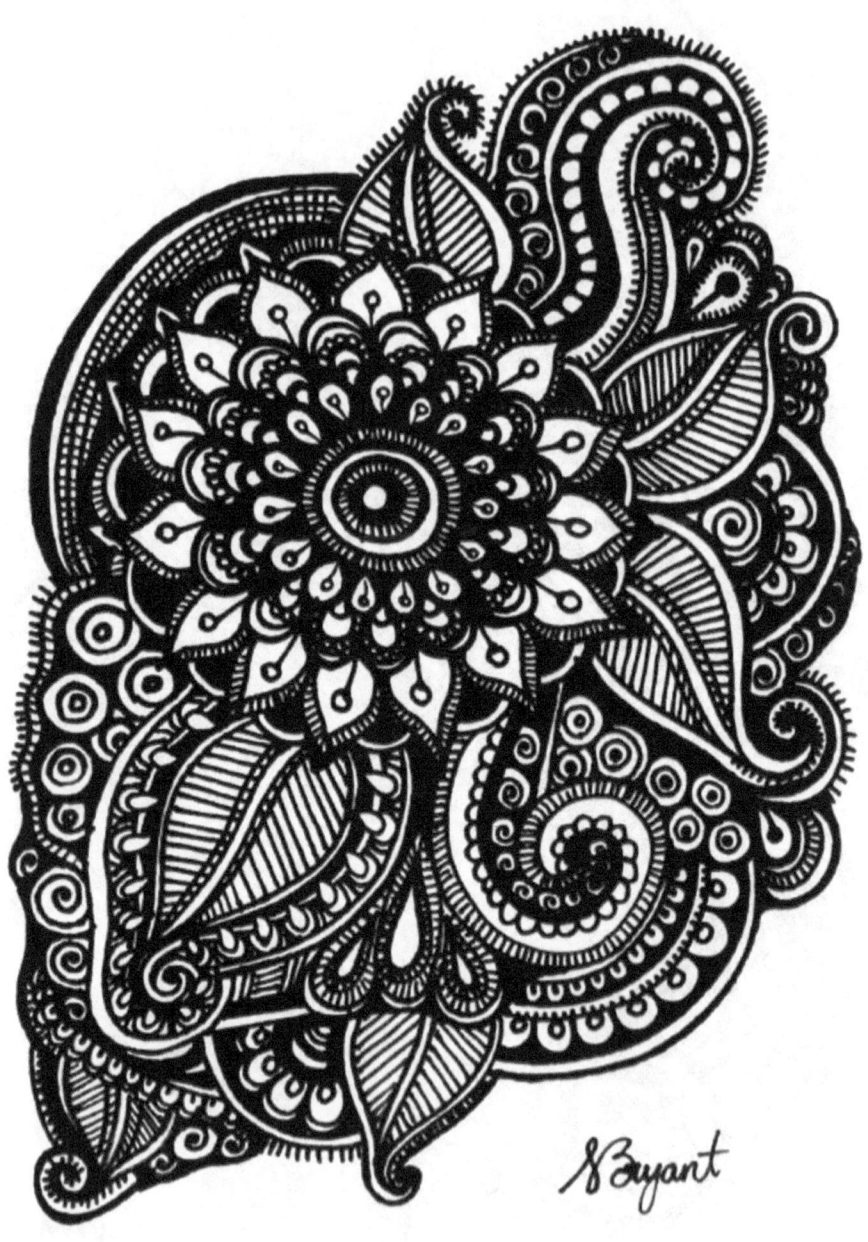

Floral Bloom

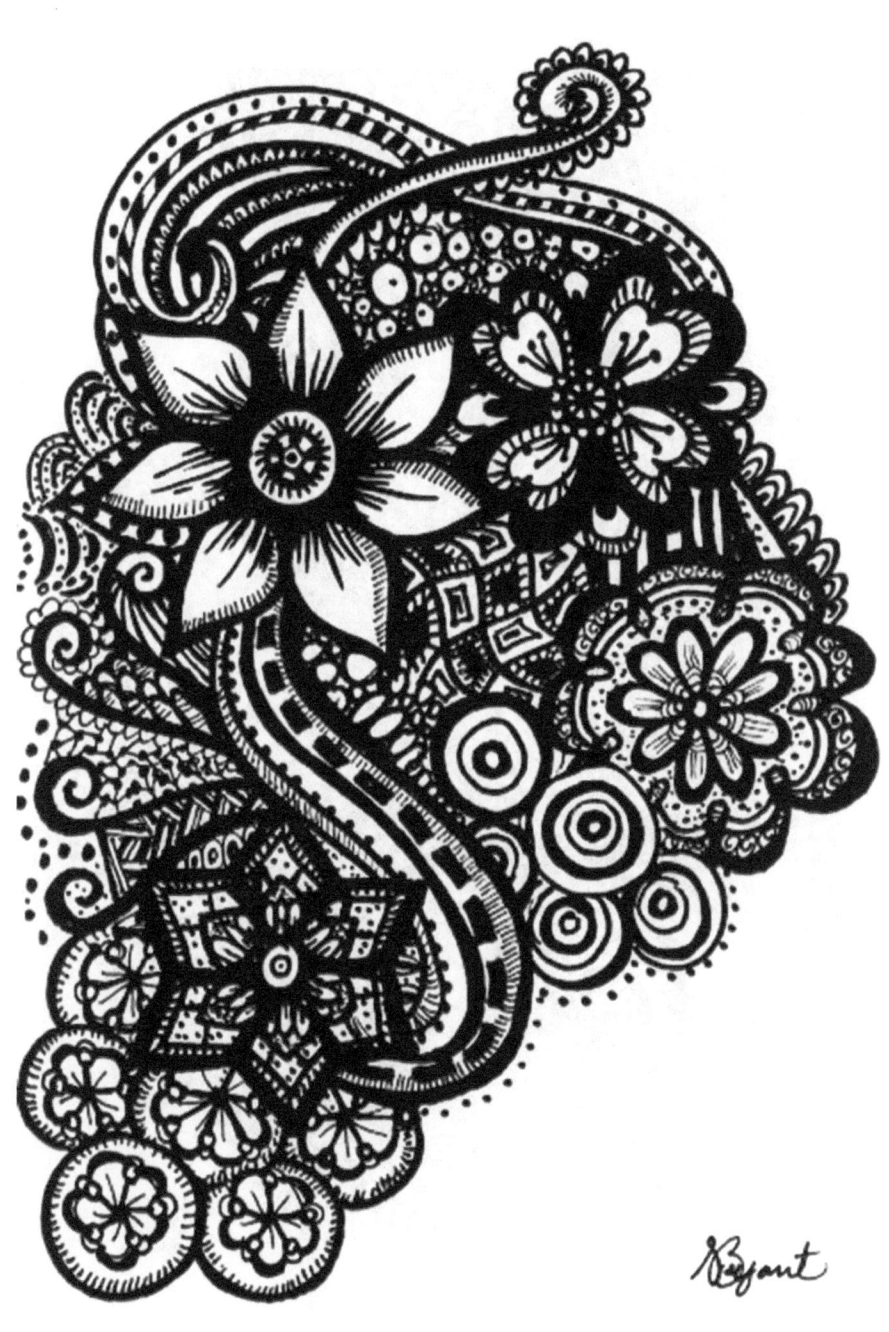

Floral Cone

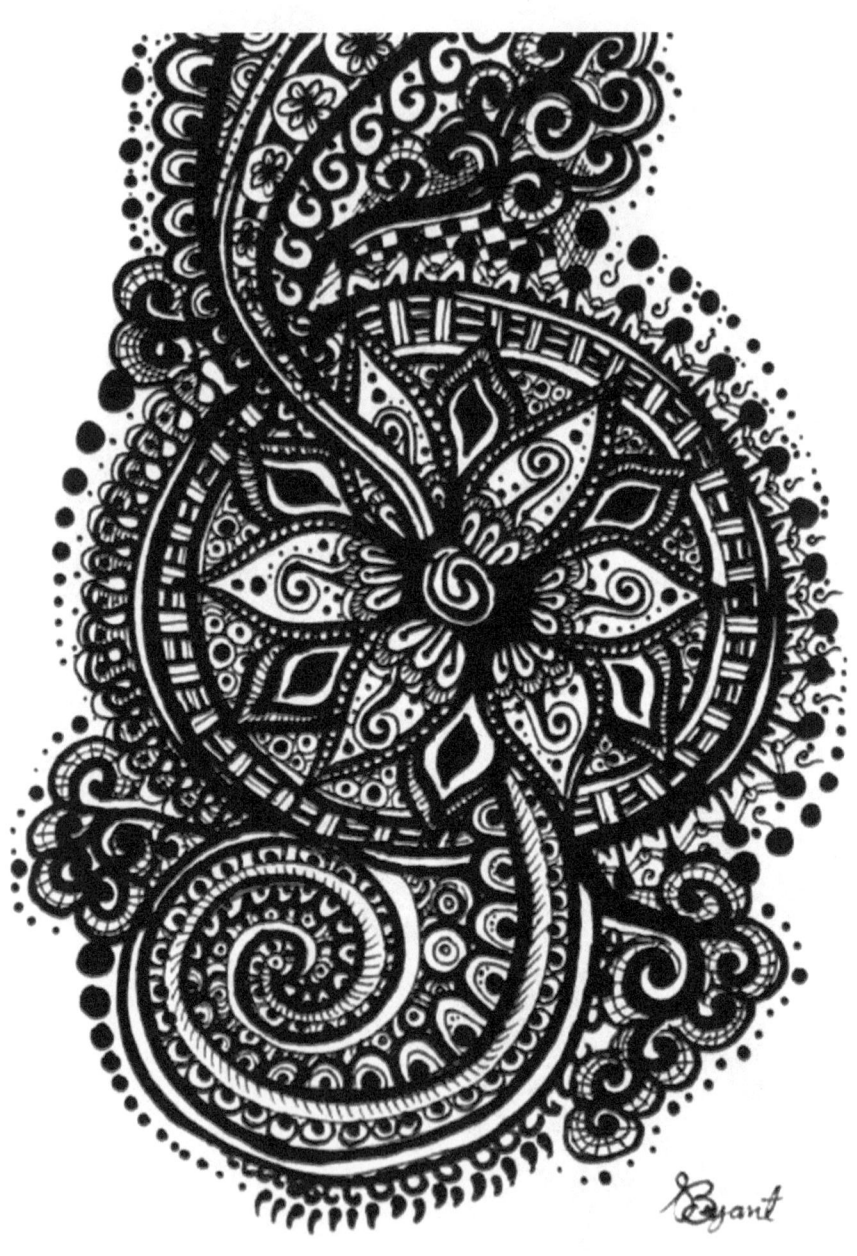

Flower Wheel

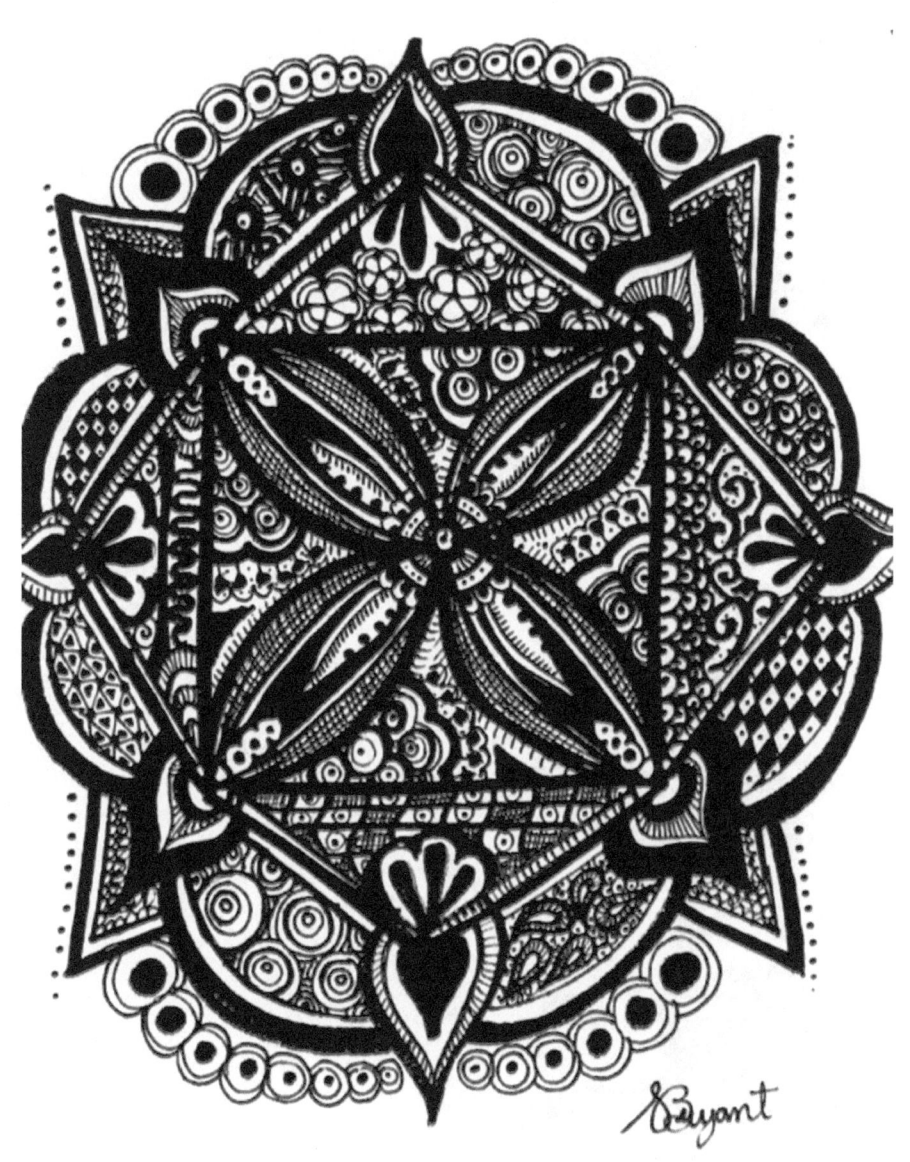

Bryant

Four Corners

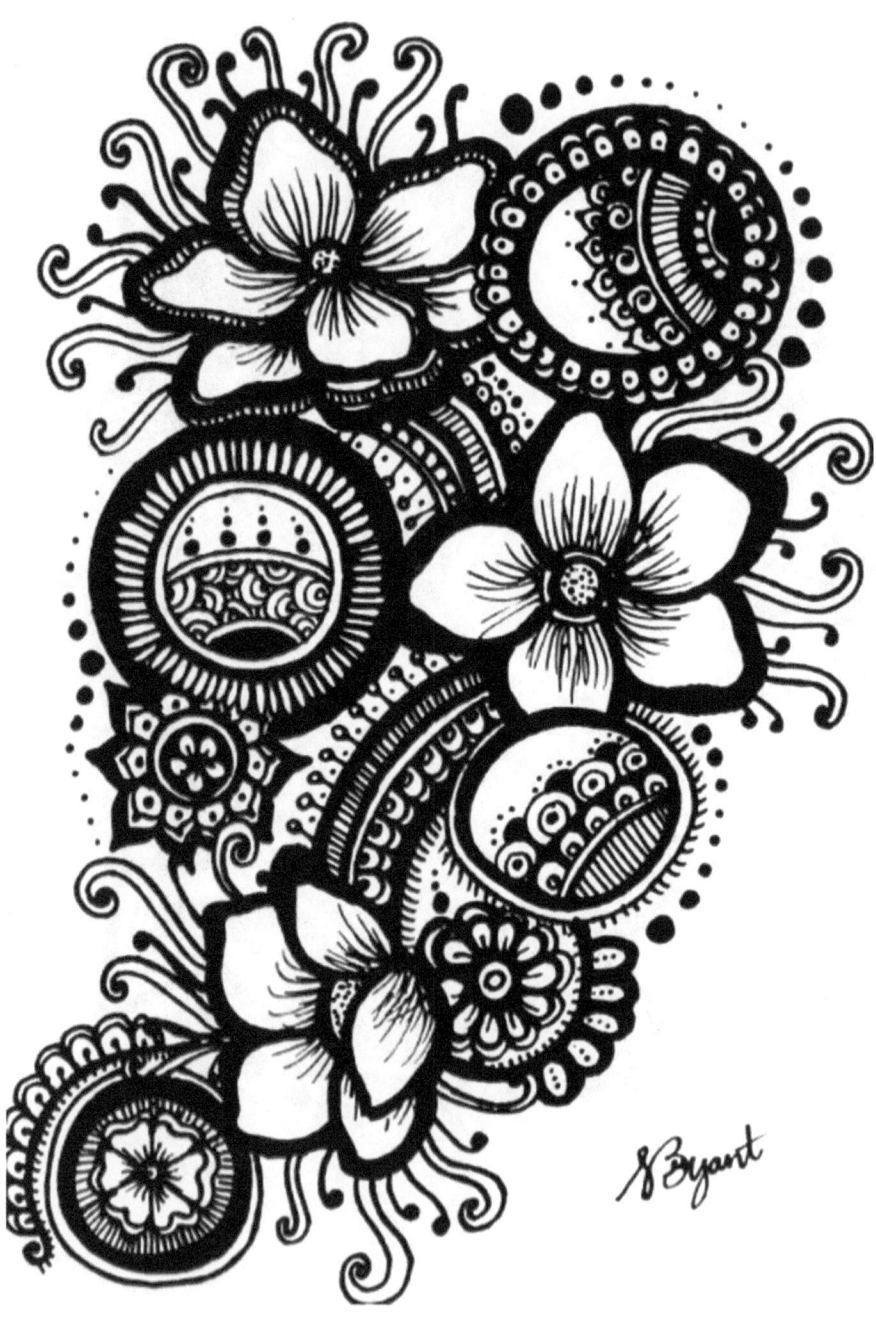

Gifts of Nature

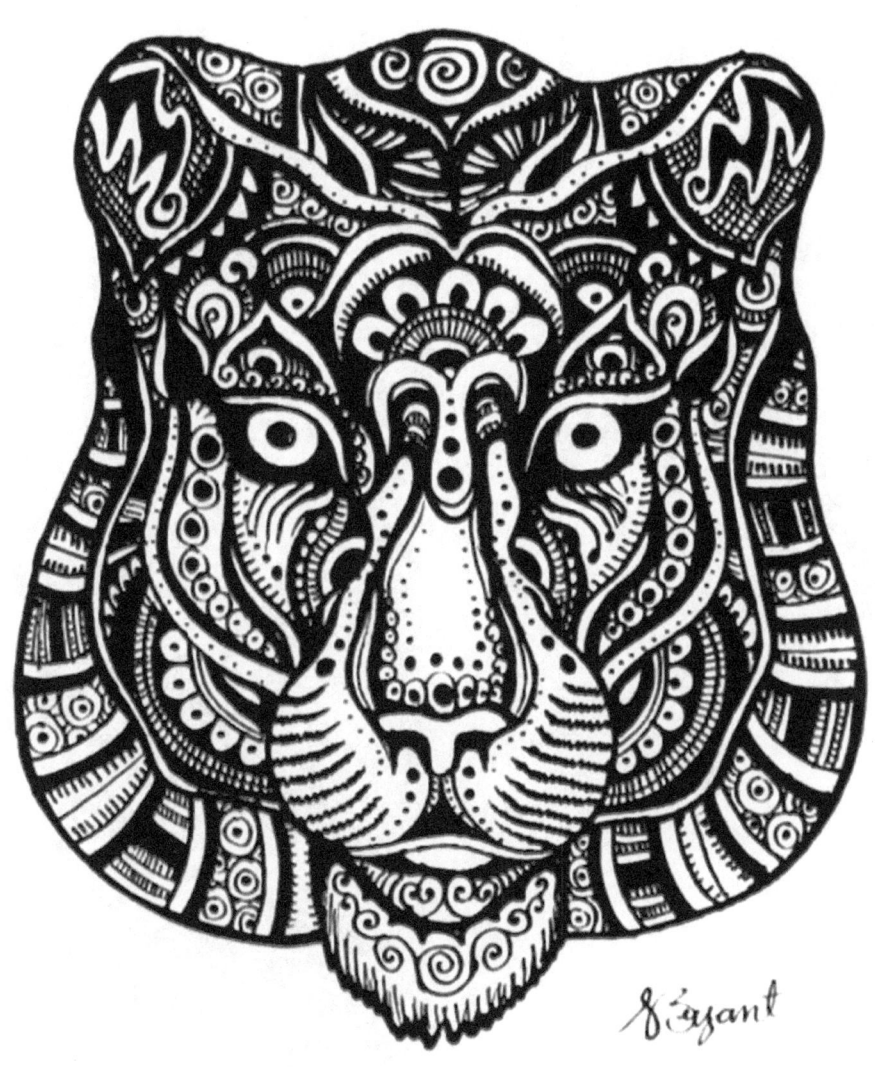

He Sees You

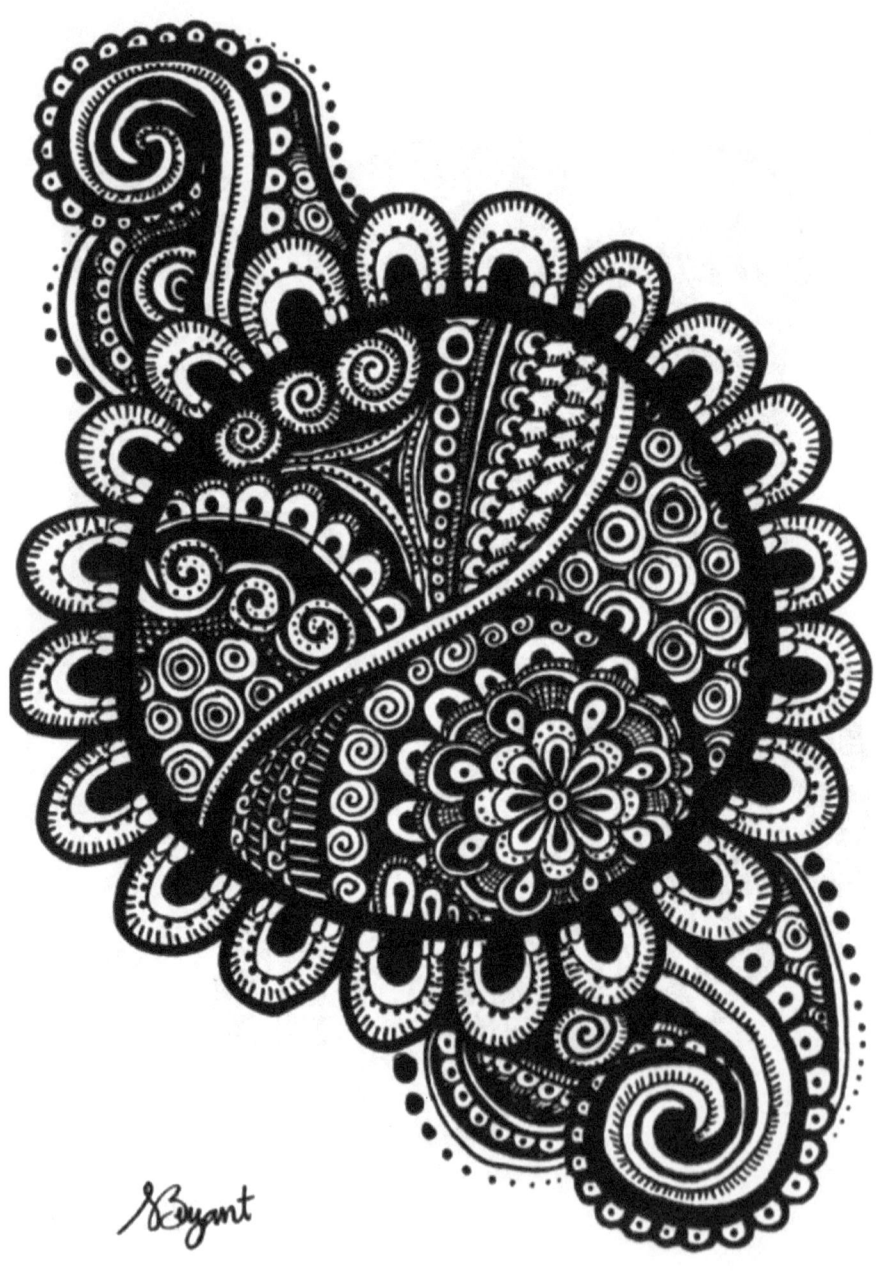

Bryant

In Balance

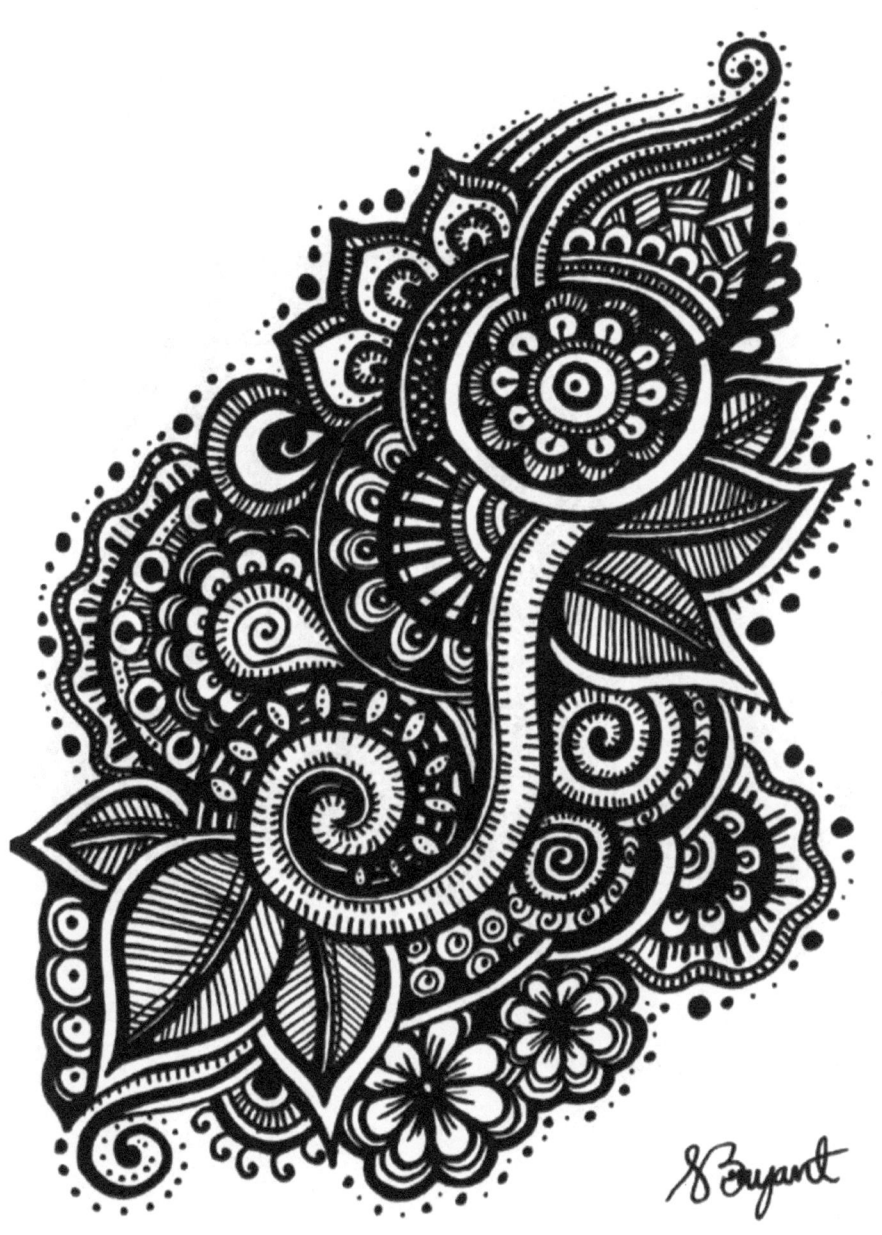

Komorebi

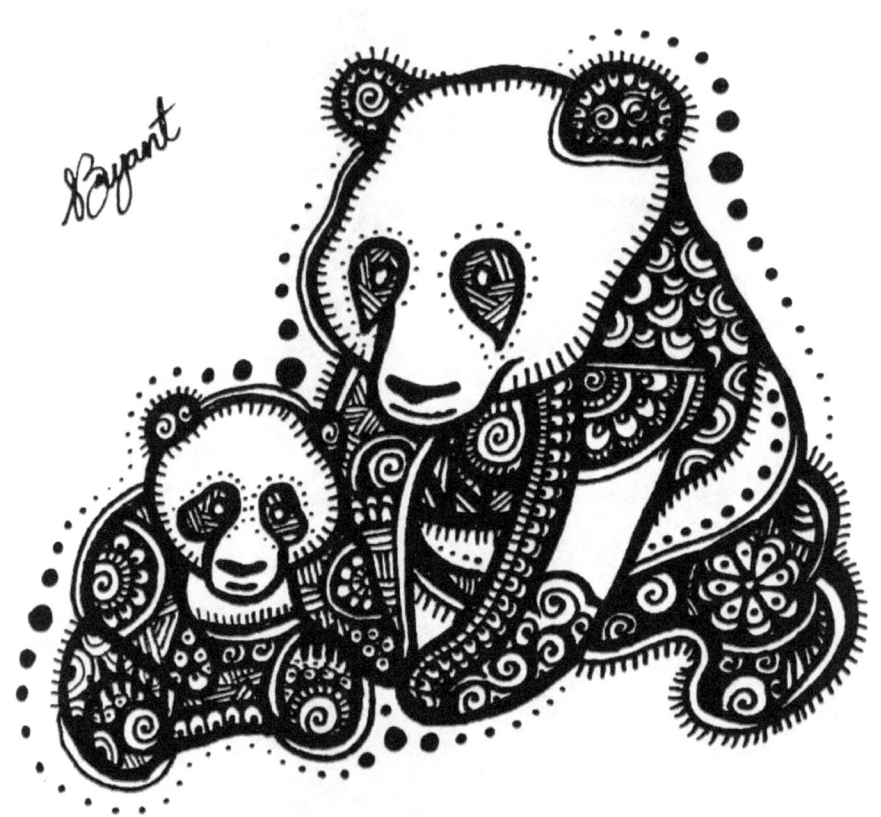

Bryant

Mother and Cub

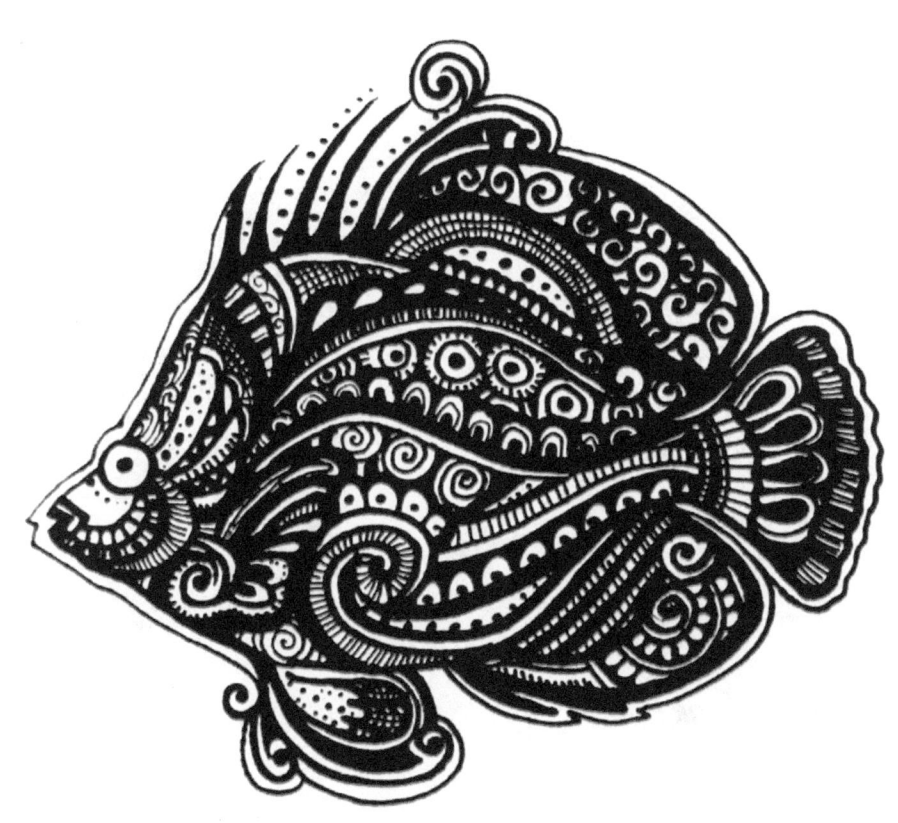

Nandi

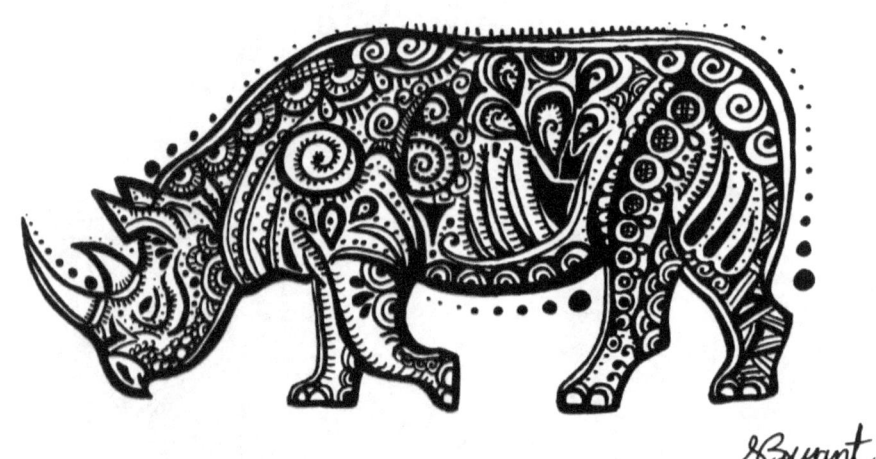

SBryant

Nature's Tank

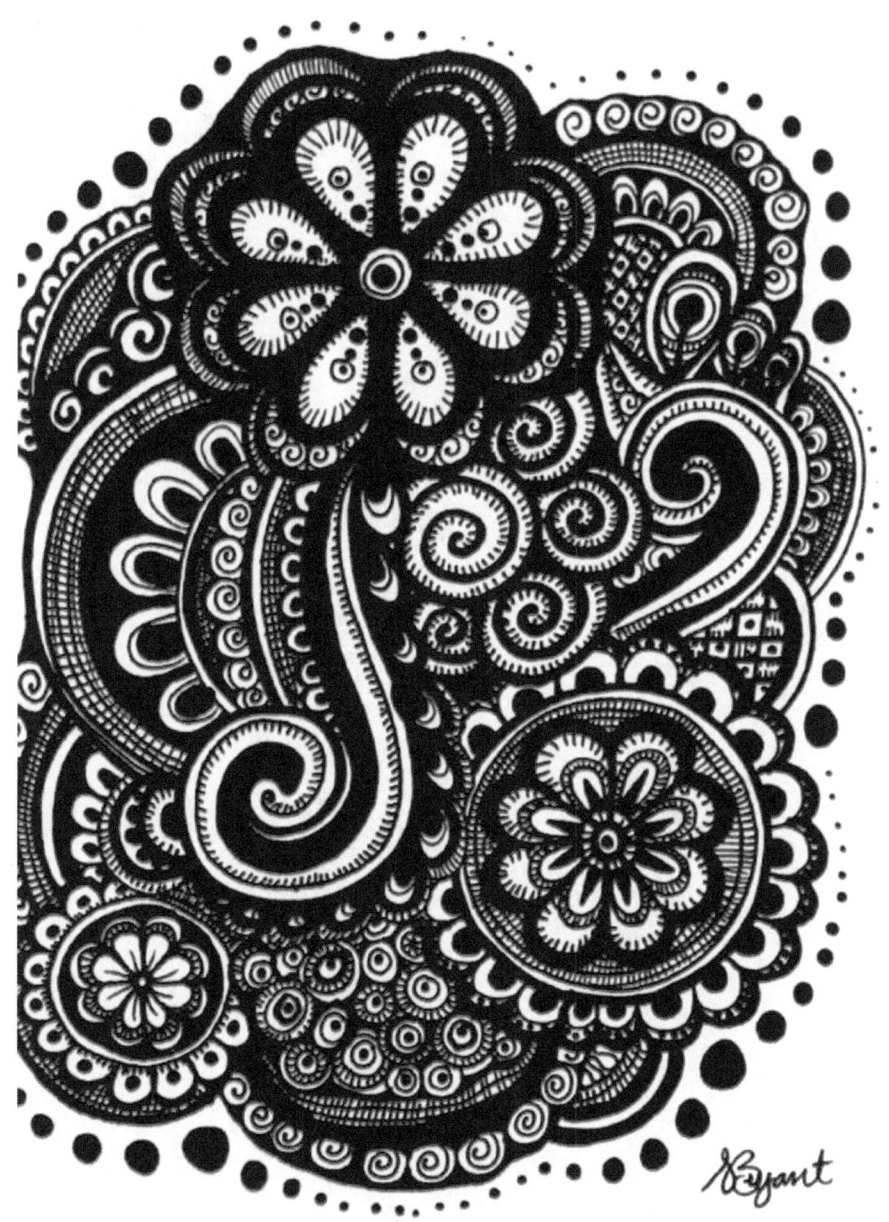

New Life

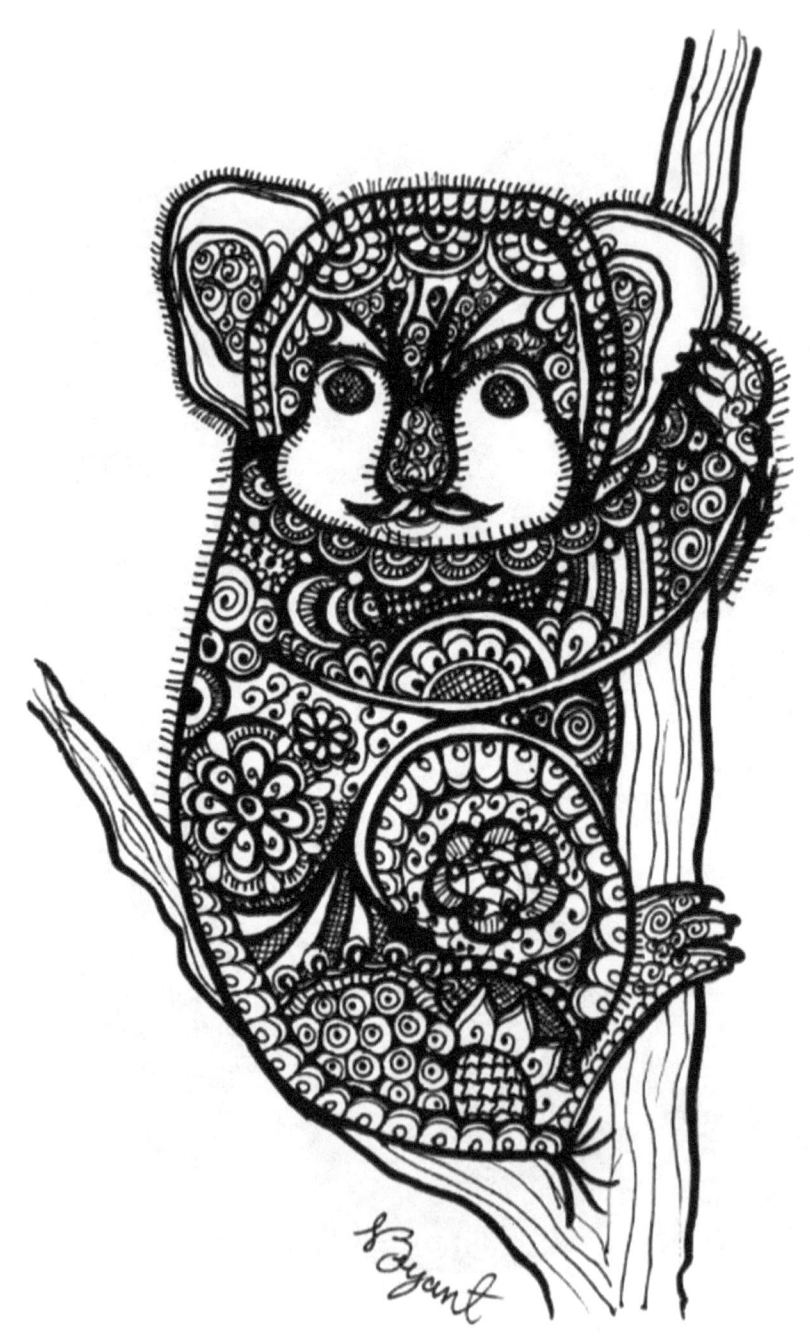

Perched in a Tree

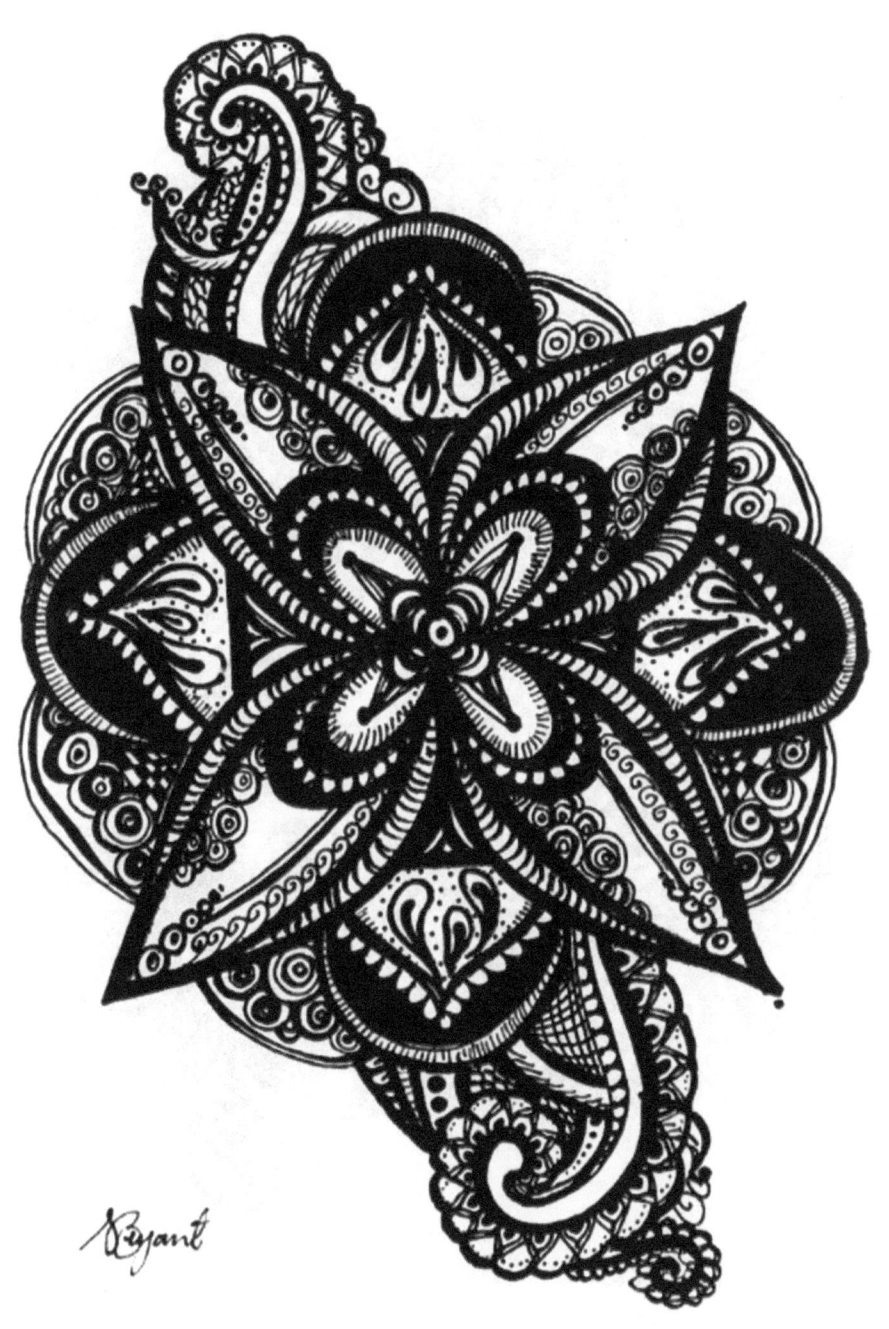

Petal Burst

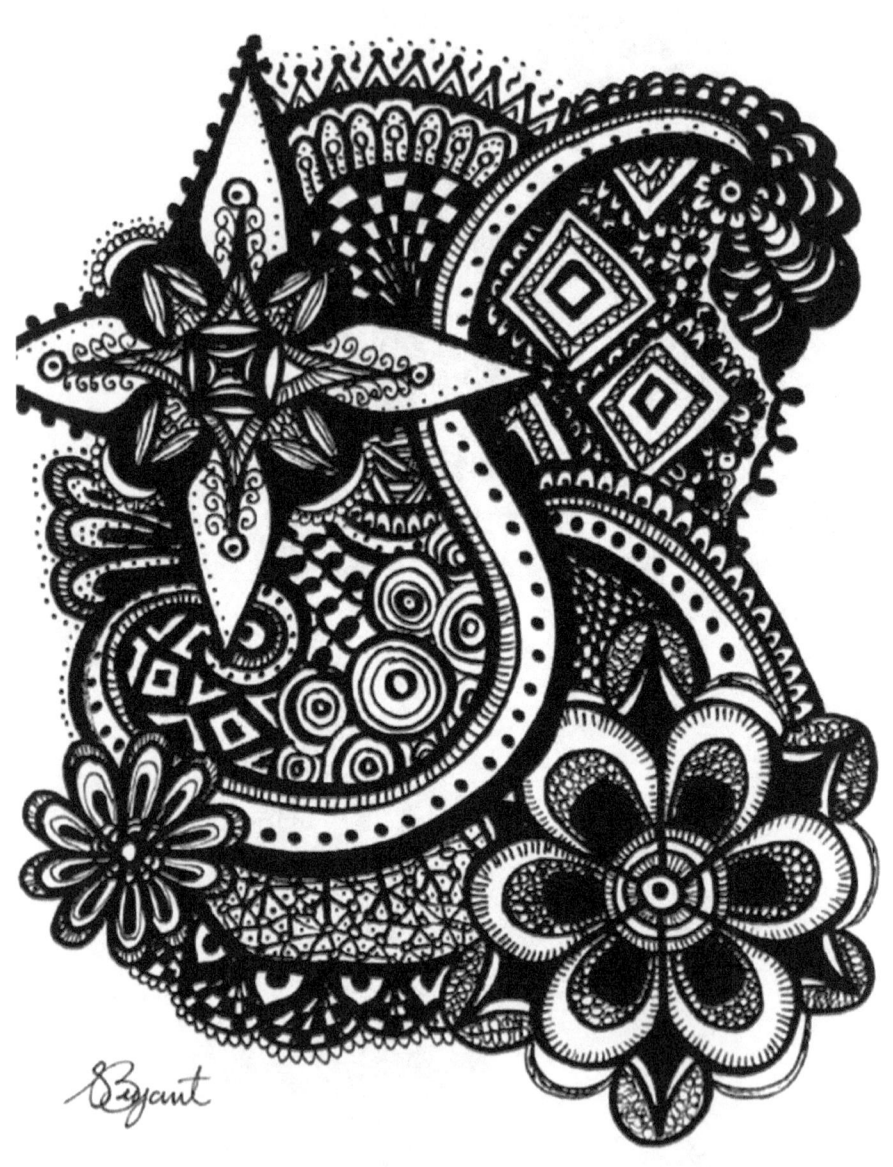

Points and Curves

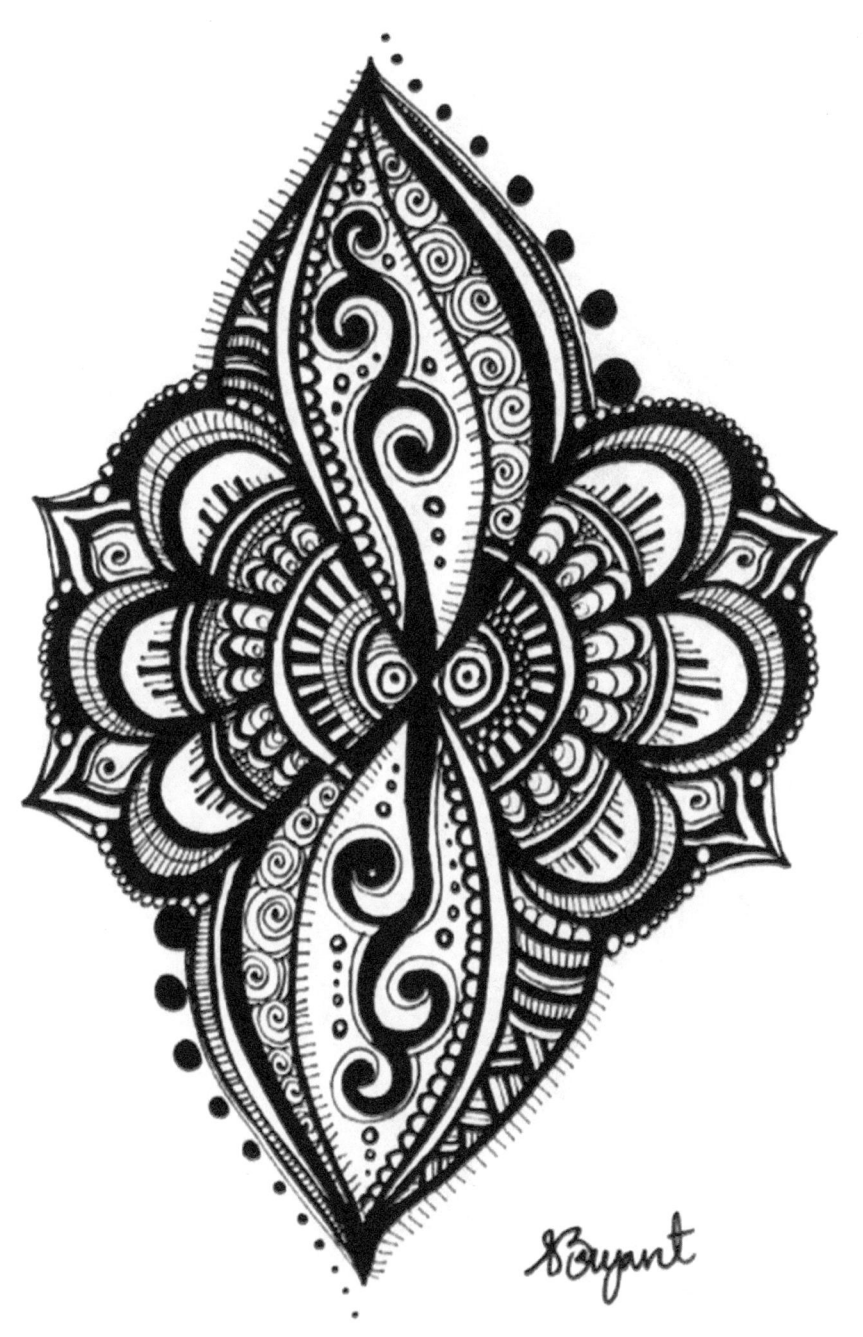

Bryant

Propel

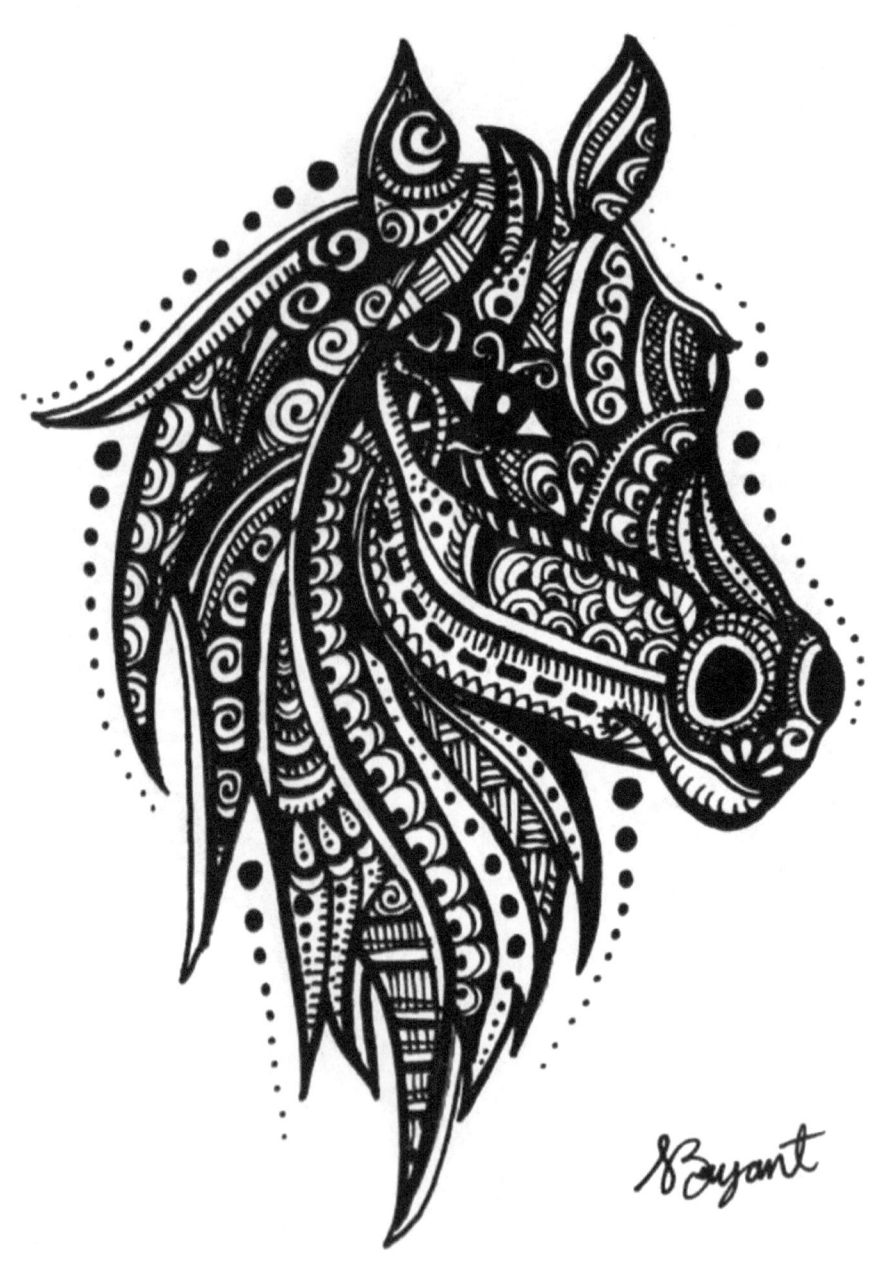

Regal Queen

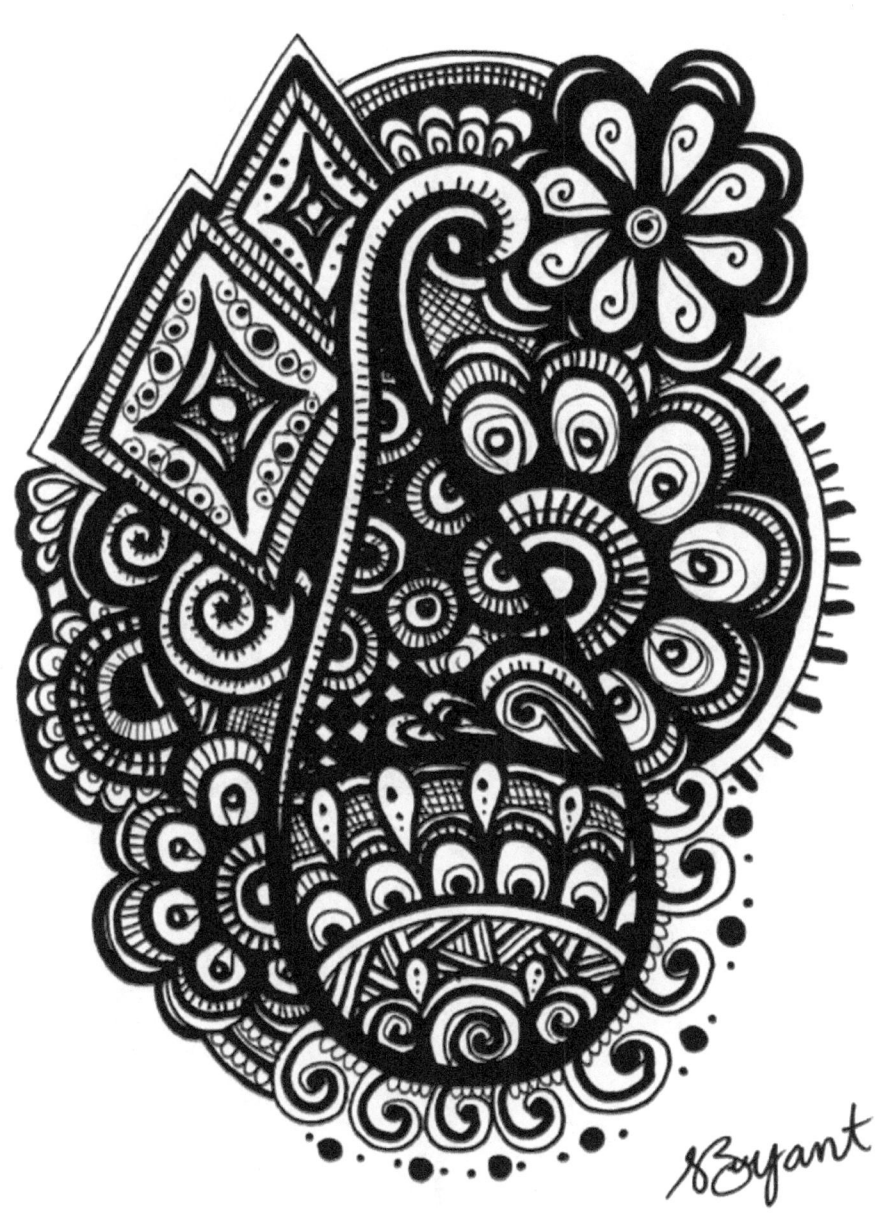

Bryant

Release the Genie

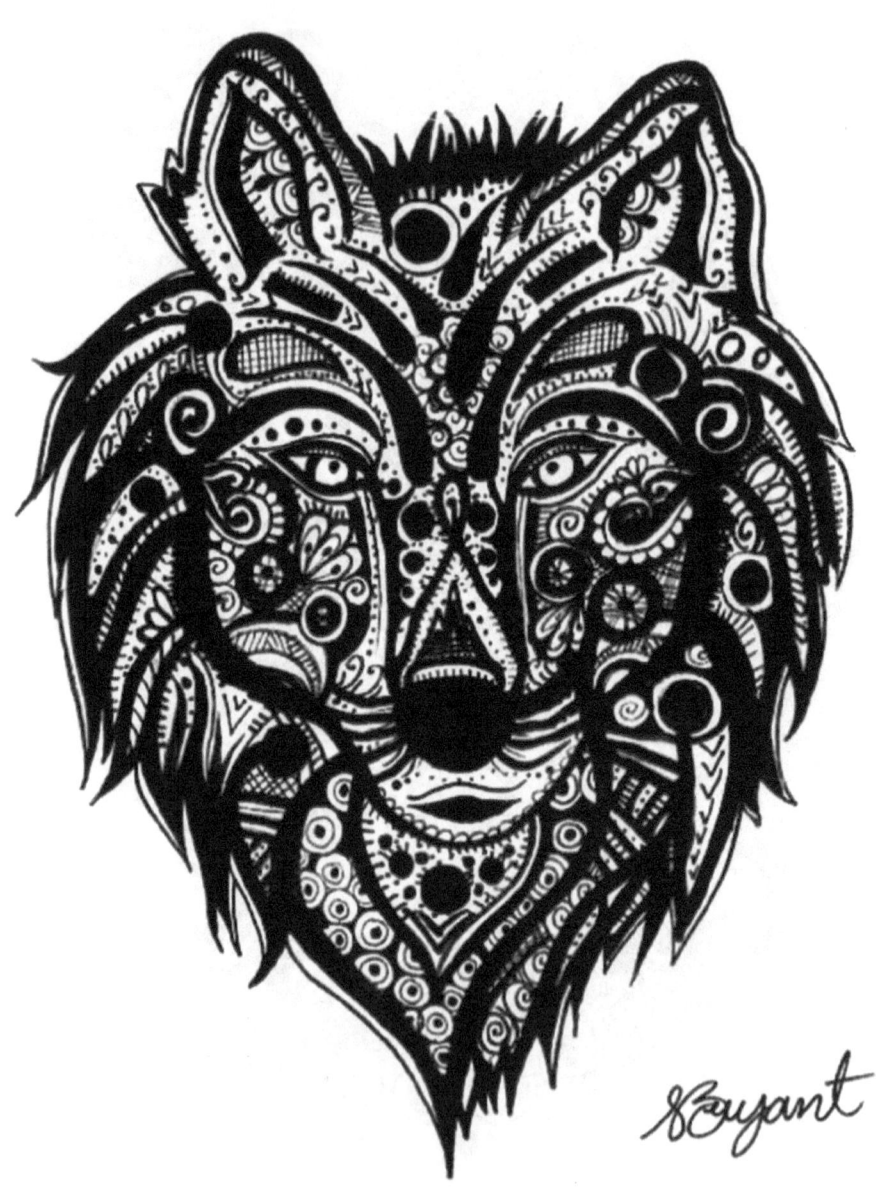

She-wolf

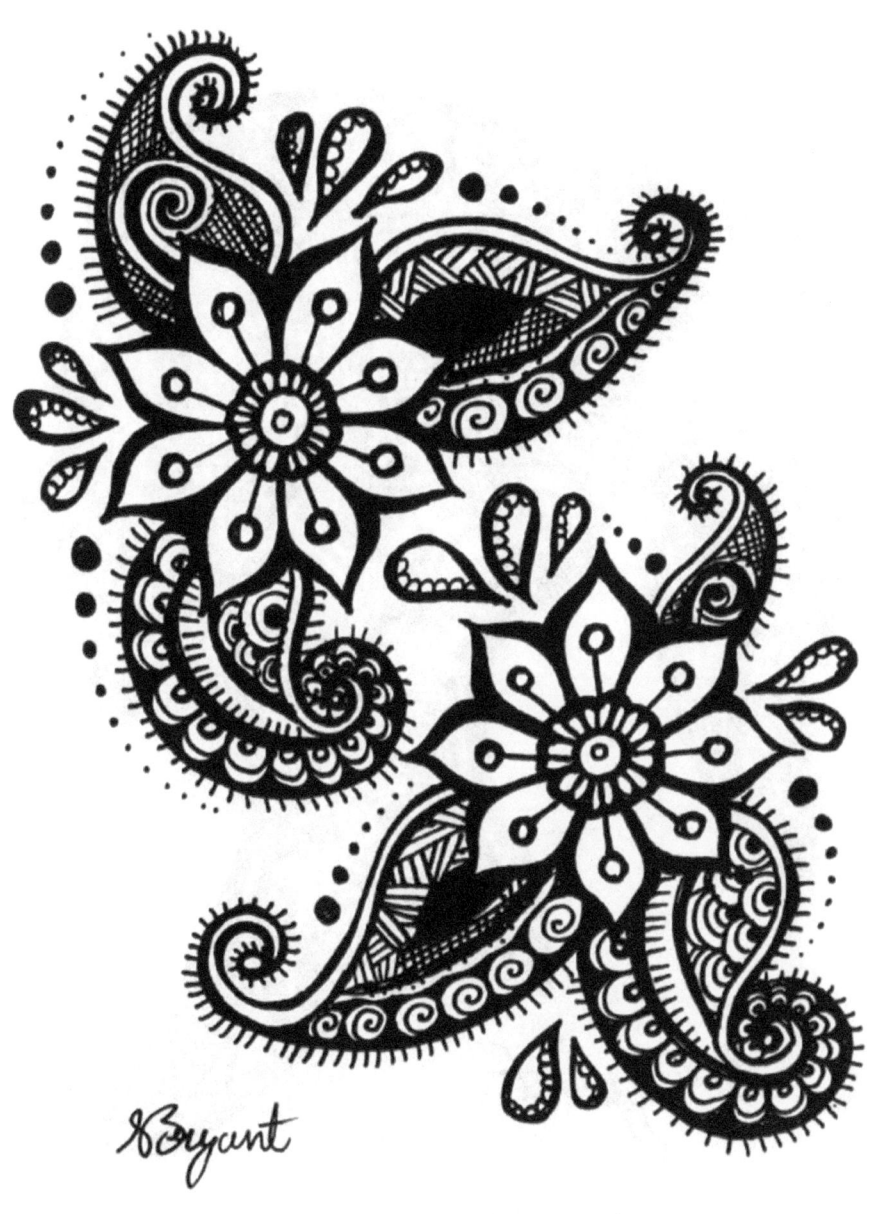

Siamese Flowers

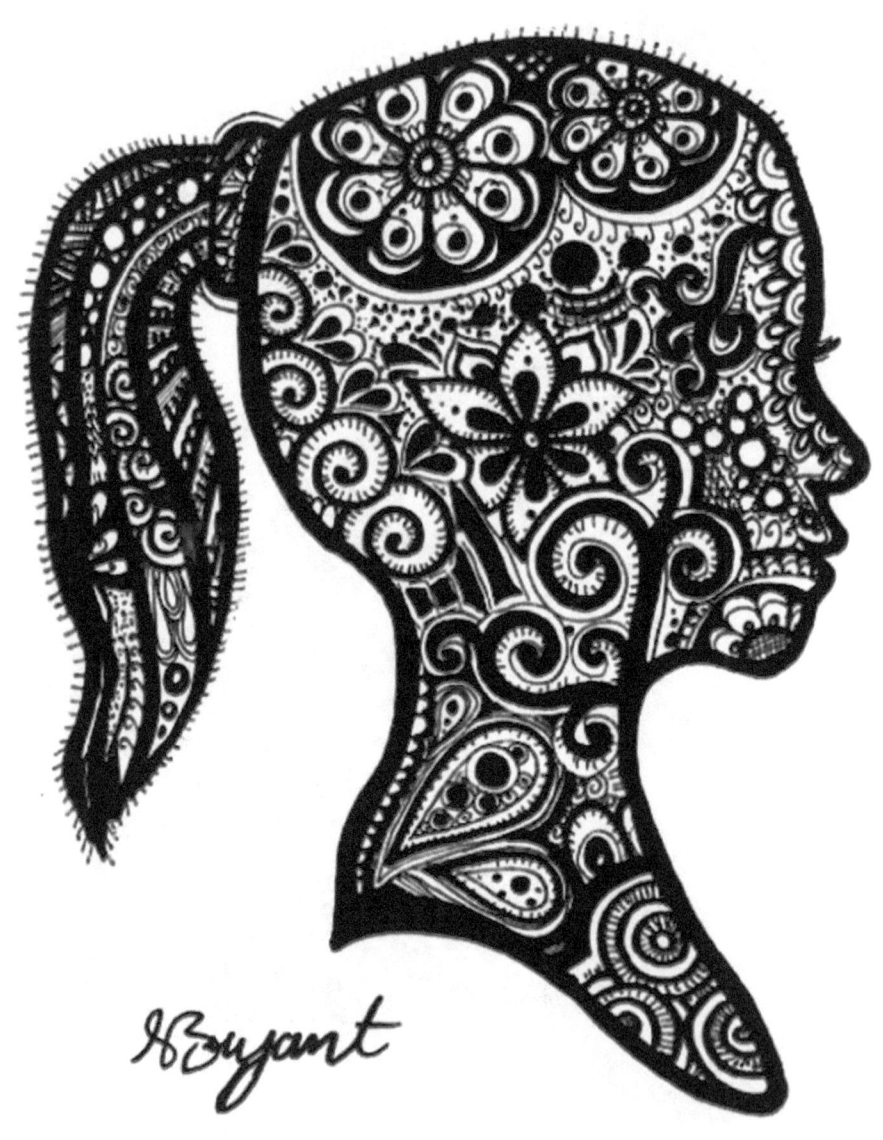

Silhouette

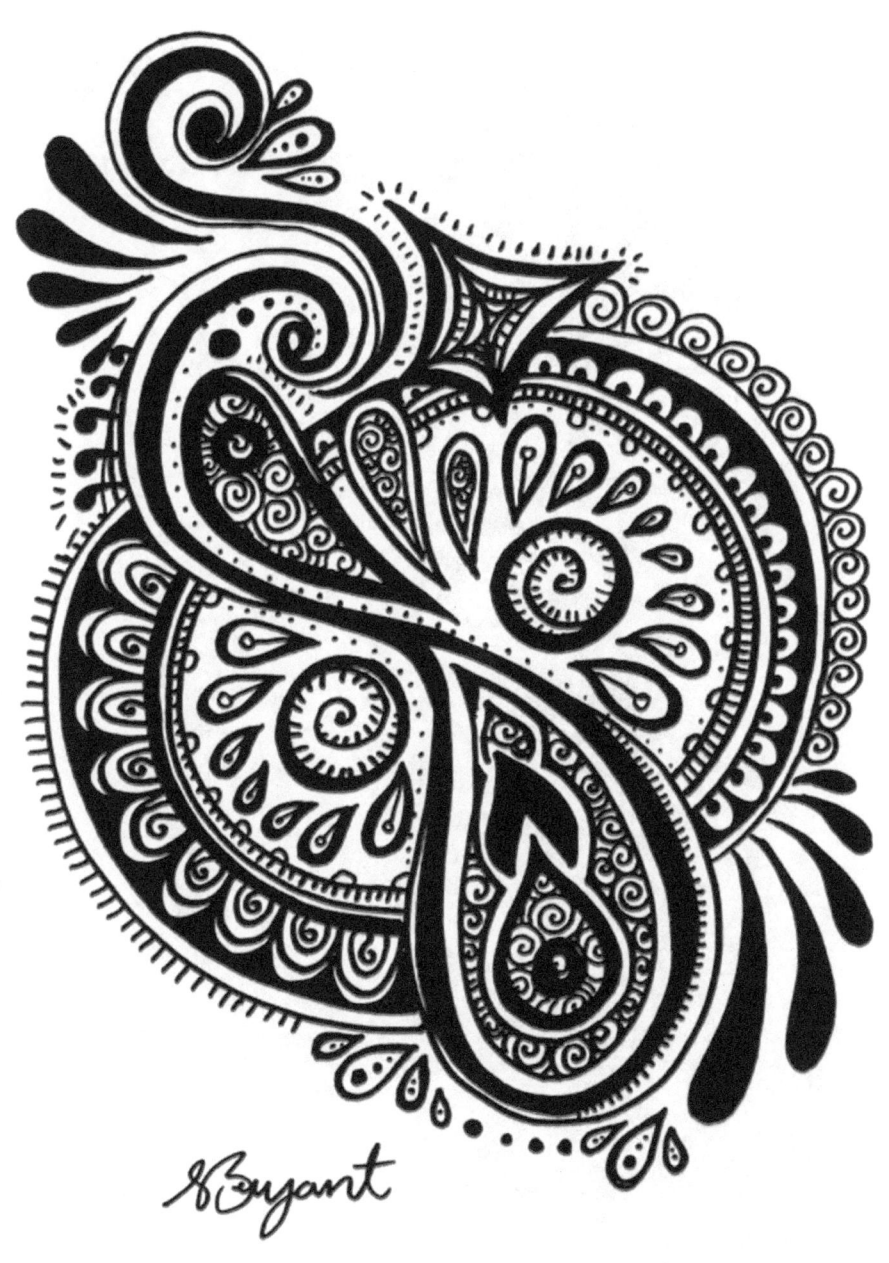

Splash

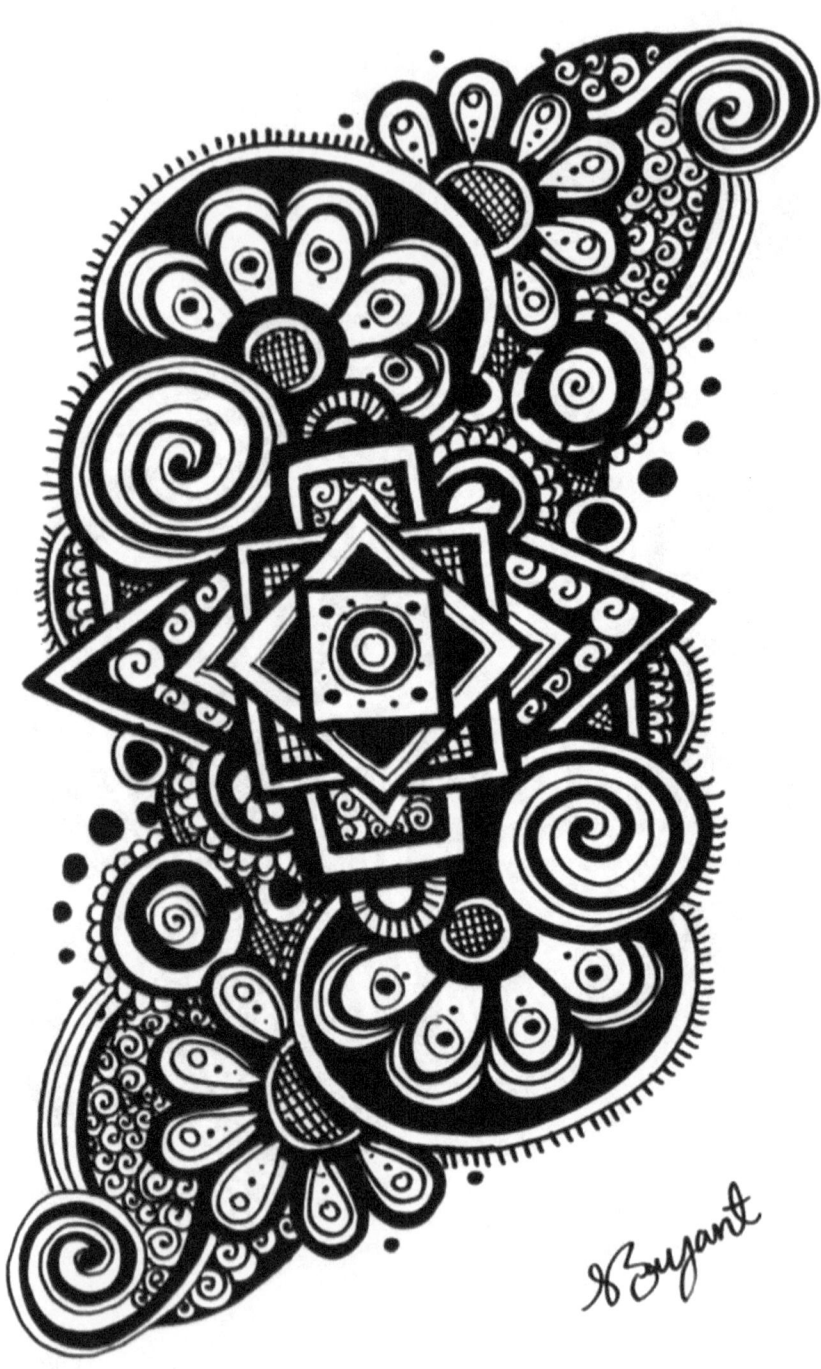

Tail Feathers

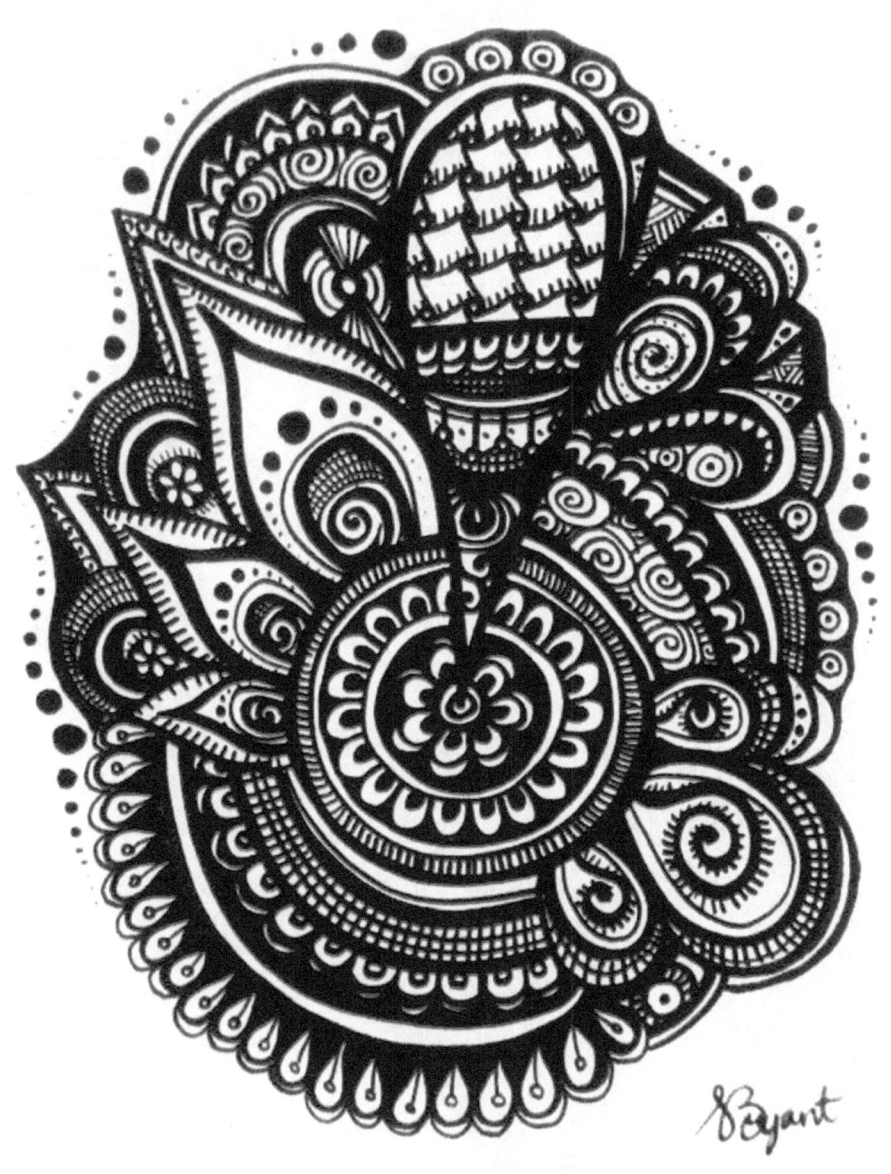

Taj

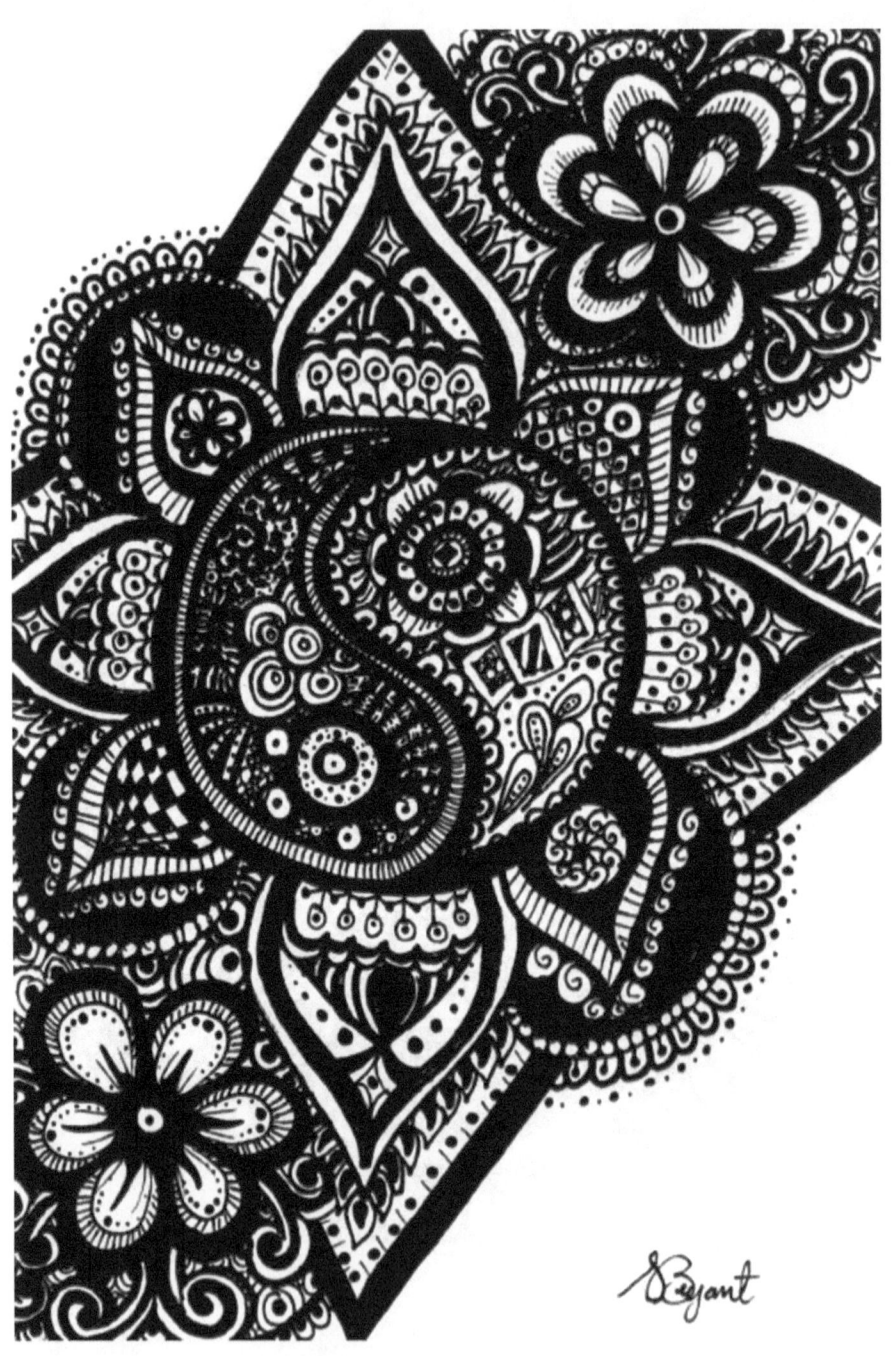

The Balance of Opposites

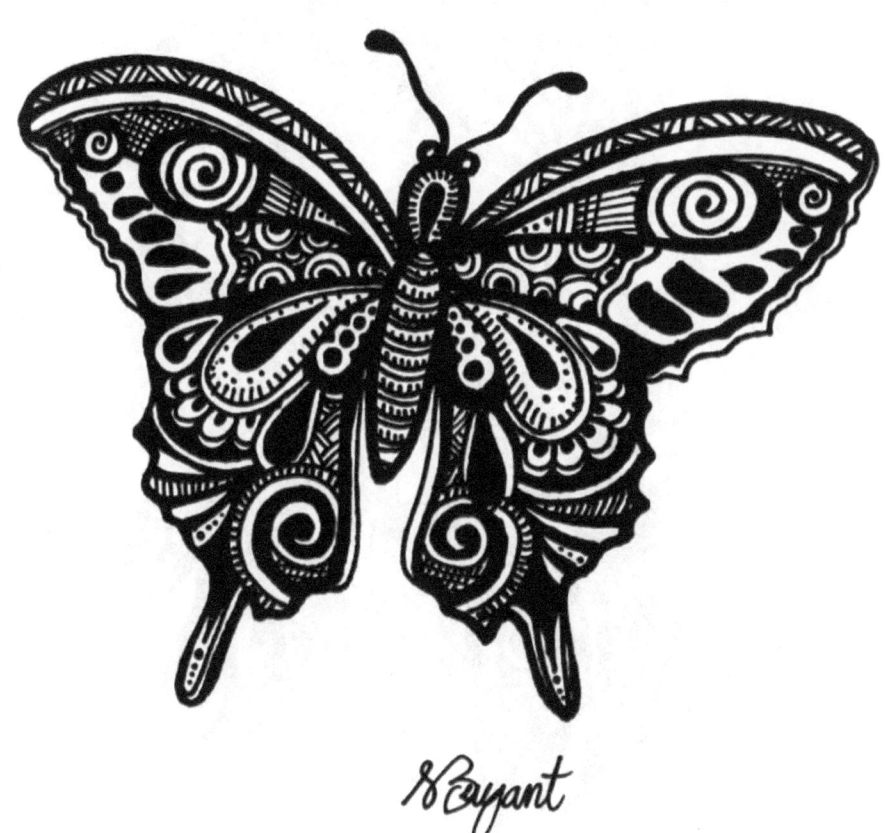

N Bryant

The Caterpillar's Released

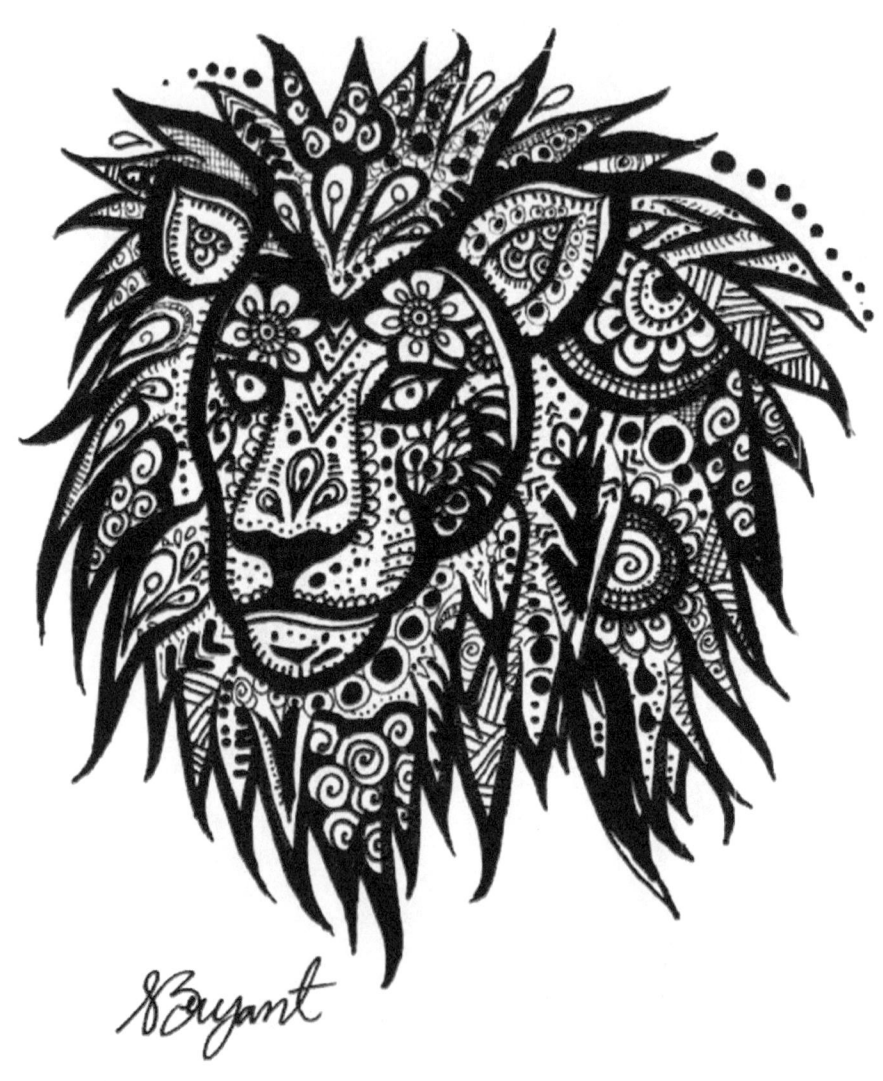

The King

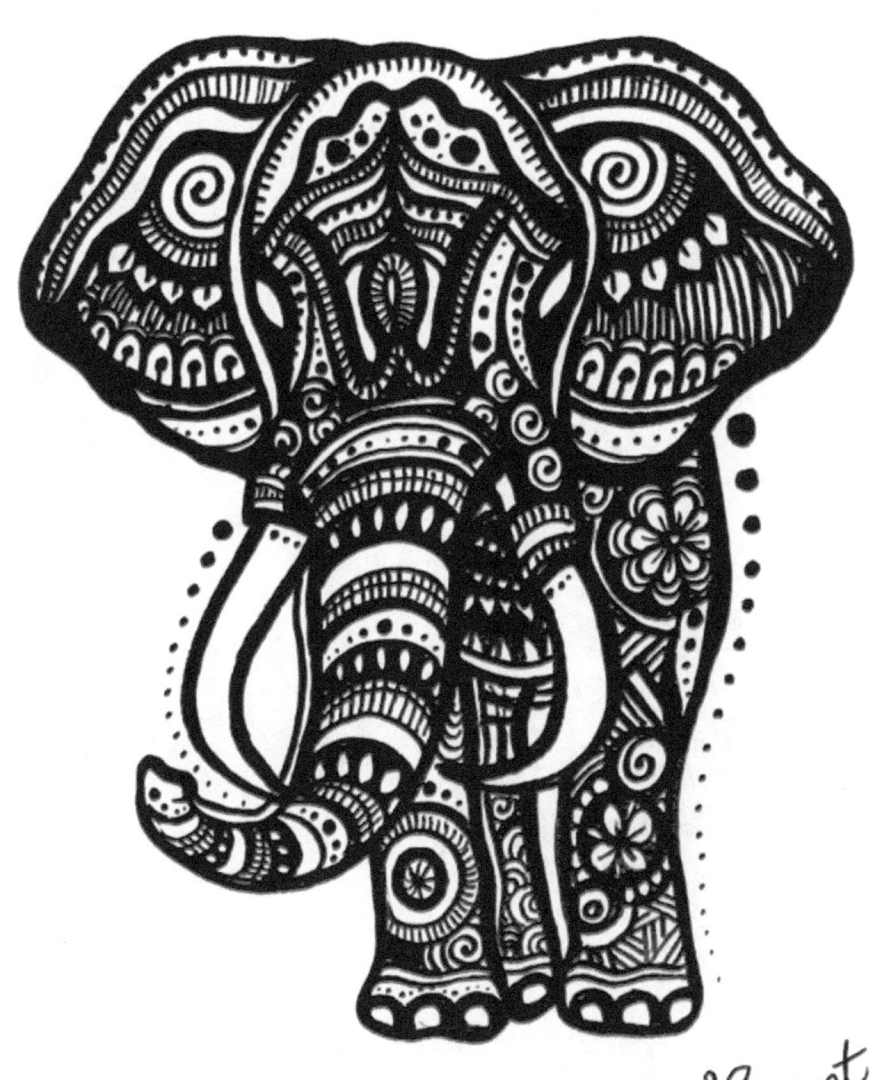

Bryant

The Mightly Elephant

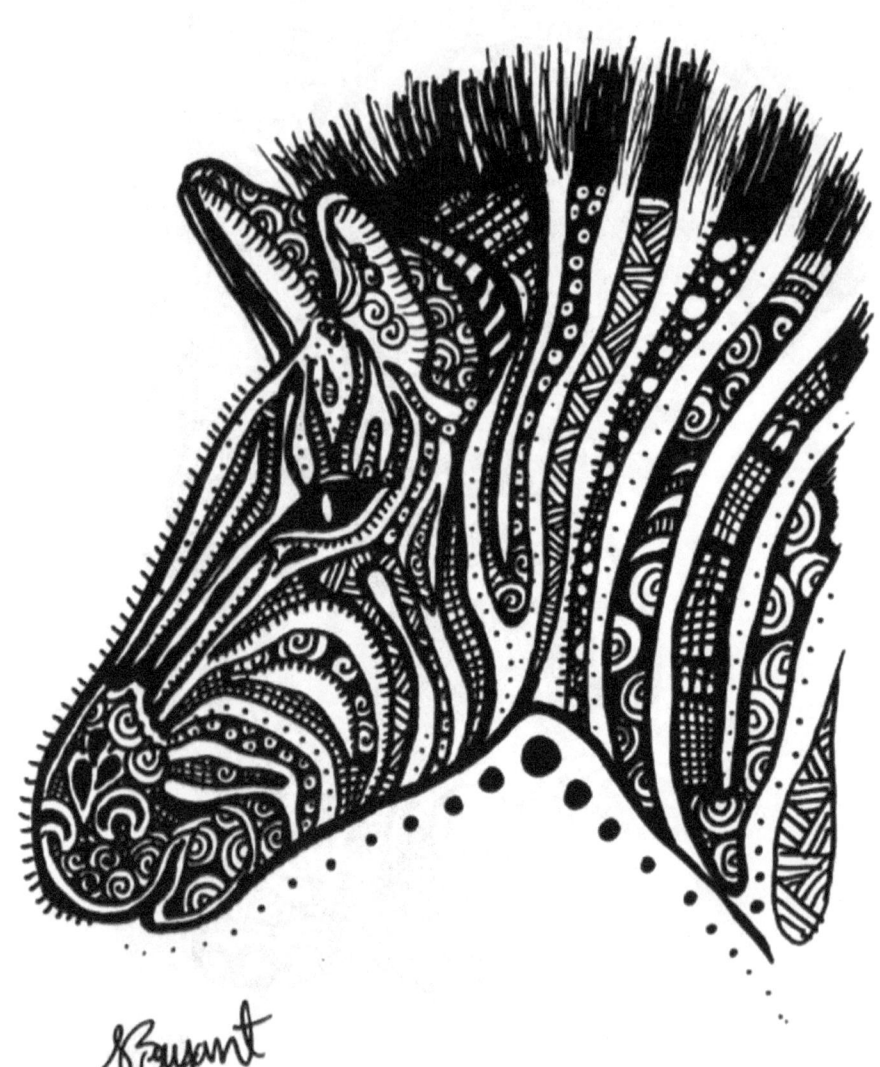

The Striped Stallion

46

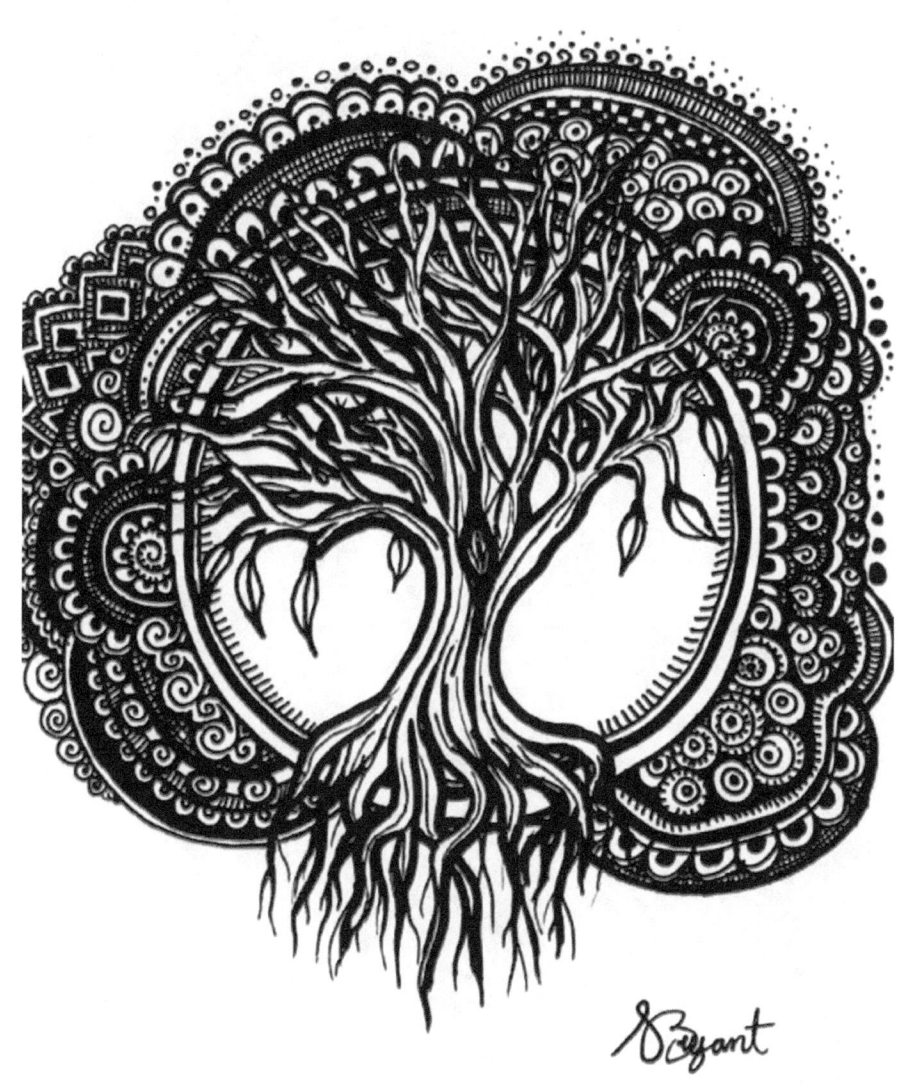

Bryant

The Tree of Life

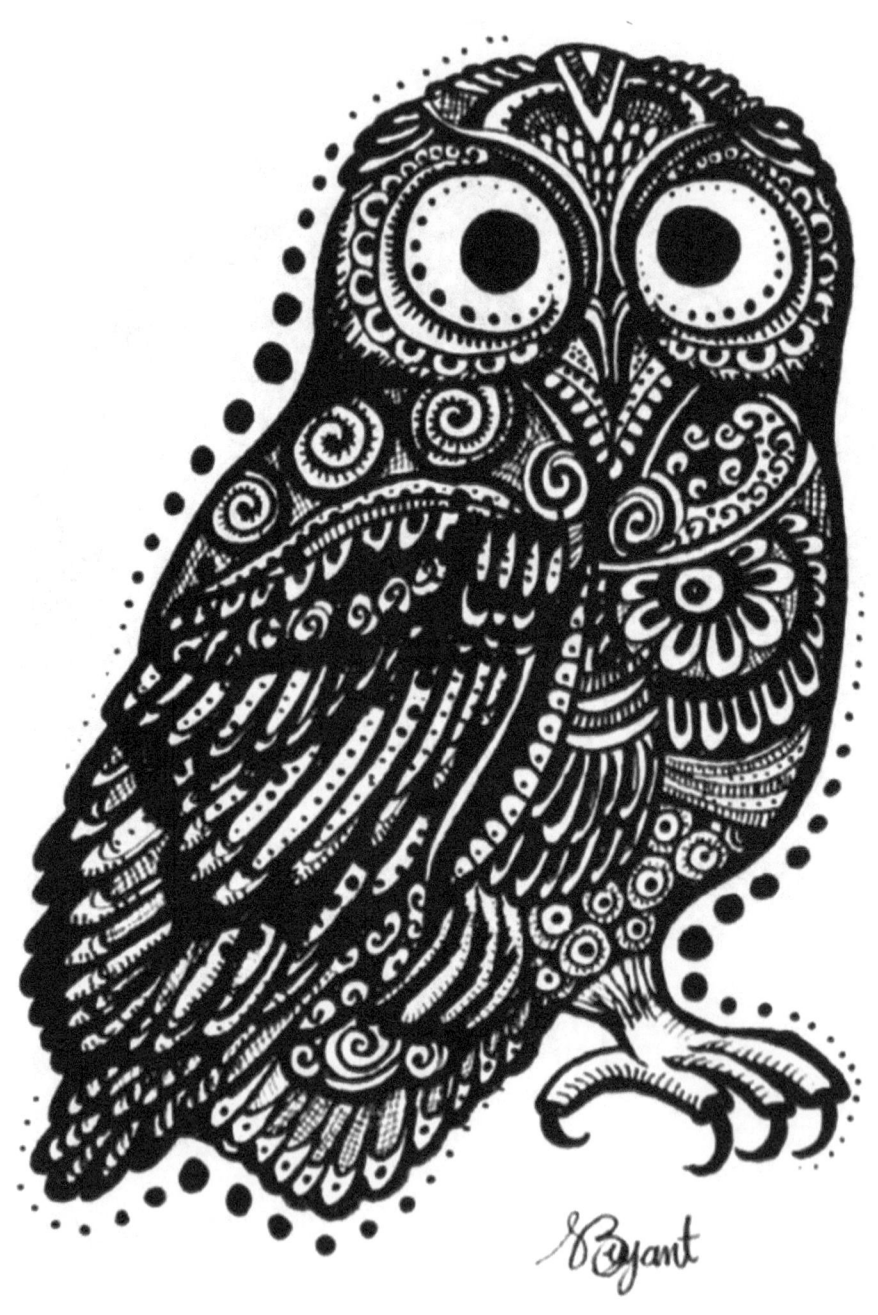

The Wise Owl

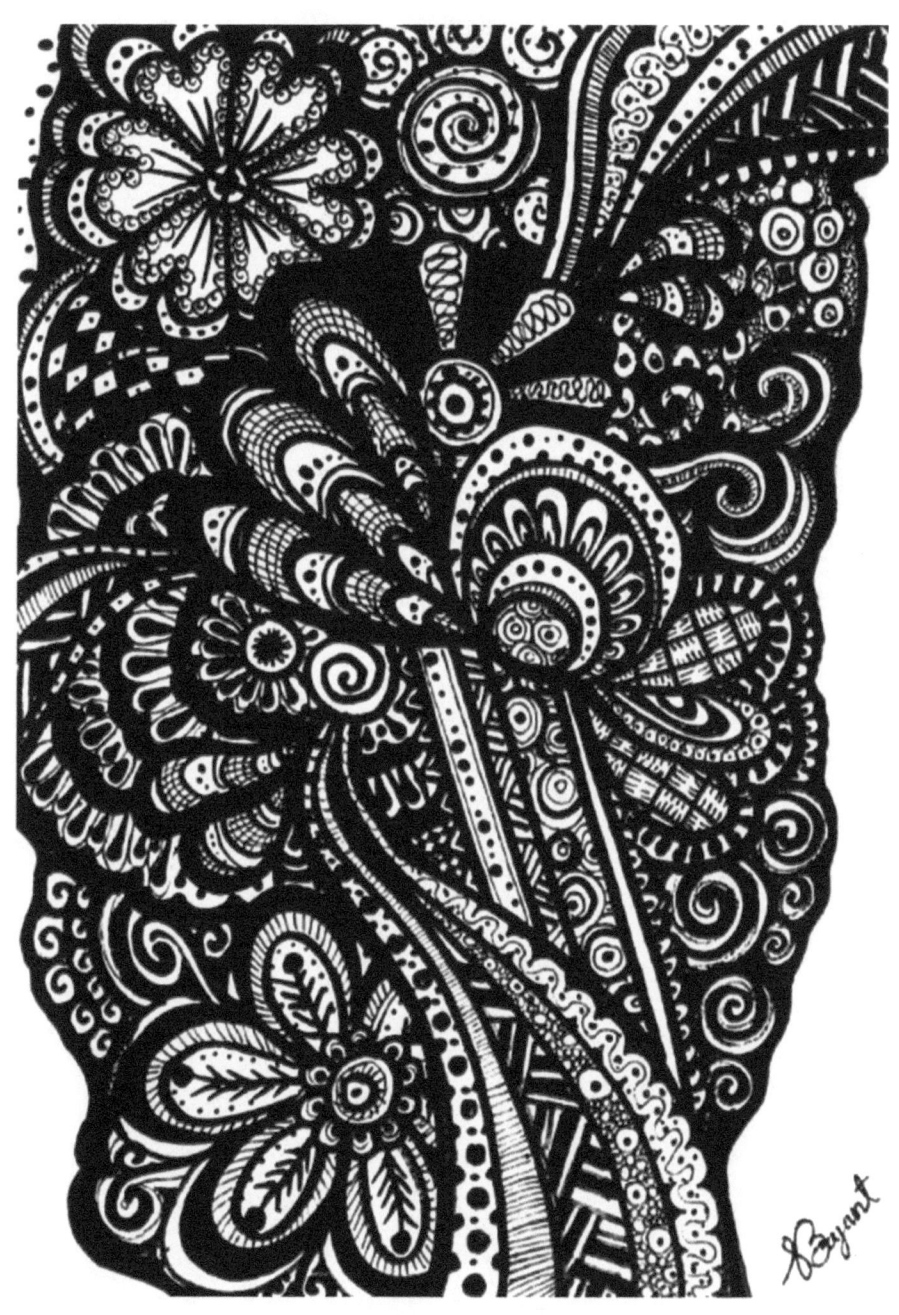

Waterfall of Patterns